COOKING WITH
Bon Appétit

COOKING WITH
Bon Appétit

Pasta and Pizza

THE KNAPP PRESS
Publishers
Los Angeles

Published by The Knapp Press
5900 Wilshire Boulevard, Los Angeles, California 90036

Library of Congress Cataloging in Publication Data

Main entry under title:

Pasta and pizza.

(Cooking with Bon appétit)
Includes index.
1. Cookery (Macaroni). 2. Pizza. I. Bon appétit.
II. Series.
TX809.M17P356 1985 641.8'22 85-9829
ISBN 0-89535-167-6

On the cover: *Capellini with Fresh Tomato and Basil Sauce*

Printed and bound in the United States of America

10 9 8 7 6 5 4 3 2 1

Contents

Foreword vii

1 Basic and Specialty Pastas . . . 1

2 Pasta with Butter, Cheese and Cream Sauces 11

3 Pasta with Vegetables and Herbs 21

4 Pasta with Seafood 55

5 Pasta with Poultry and Meat 67

6 Oriental Noodles 87

7 Pizza 97

Index 113

Foreword

Remember when *pasta* meant spaghetti and meatballs? When pizza came in three versions—cheese, meatball and pepperoni? Well, all that has changed dramatically in the last few years. Pasta and pizza lend themselves to endless variation, and these days inventive cooks everywhere are taking full advantage of their wonderful adaptability.

Now that both hand-operated and electric pasta machines are widely available, pasta is turning up in a spectrum of colors and flavors that are news even to the most sophisticated. In this volume you will find pastas flavored with broccoli, green peas, red pepper, saffron, tomato, green onion—even lemon and orange. The simplest "sauce"—a drizzle of butter and a sprinkling of cheese—is all these flavored versions really need, but with the full-dress treatment of a meat, seafood or vegetable sauce they are very special indeed.

There is also no limit to the dishes you can prepare using commercially made pasta. Pair store-bought fettuccine and linguine with opulently rich sauces based on Gorgonzola, mascarpone and other cheeses; try quick, light herb and vegetable toppings on fusilli or shell macaroni; team substantial meat, poultry and seafood mixtures with ziti and rigatoni.

Whether you use purchased or handmade pasta, get acquainted with its myriad forms. It comes in simple strands and intricate shapes; it can be rolled, molded, stuffed or baked; it may be served hot or cold, as a first course or main dish. And don't forget the array of distinctive noodles available at oriental markets: Japanese *udon,* buckwheat *soba,* rice sticks, bean threads. They are all in this book, in classic dishes and intriguing new combinations.

Pizza is just as versatile. The chapter includes several shortcut recipes for quick family meals, but you will also find pizza spectaculars: Shrimp and Leek Pizza with Feta Cheese, Tomato-Potato Pissaladière, Mediterranean Pizza with Zucchini and Eggplant, and lots of others. Use these recipes for starters, then let your fancy be your guide; pizza is perfect for improvising.

Pasta and pizza: simple yet sophisticated, traditional yet up-to-the minute. With this selection of *Bon Appétit* recipes you will see what all the excitement is about.

1 Basic and Specialty Pastas

Until quite recently it was rare indeed to find fresh pasta anywhere in the country. Today it seems to be popping up all over—in fine food shops, restaurants, even some supermarkets. But best of all, we have discovered the pleasure of making pasta at home.

Your pasta-making ventures need not employ any tools more complicated than a rolling pin. On the other hand, you may prefer to automate the procedure with a food processor and hand-operated rolling machine or, if you are a real enthusiast, with an electric pasta machine that does all the work from beginning to end. No matter which method you choose, you will be delighted at the perfect results obtainable with just a few ingredients—and simple, thrifty ones at that.

The recipes in this chapter use several types of flour—instant, regular all purpose, unbleached and semolina. Instant flour makes a particularly tender pasta, semolina a firm one. It won't take long to get a feel for the properties of various flours; once you do, go ahead and experiment to get just the texture and firmness you prefer. Pasta dough is forgiving, and no single formula is the one-and-only path to success.

Basic Processor Pasta

Makes 15 ounces (8 servings)

2¼ cups instant flour
3 eggs
1 teaspoon salt

Using food processor fitted with steel knife, combine all ingredients and process until dough forms ball.

Using pasta machine: On well-floured board, divide dough into 8 equal pieces. Cover with plastic wrap to prevent drying. Set rollers for widest setting. Lightly flour first piece of dough. Run through rollers once. Flour lightly, fold into thirds and run through rollers again. Repeat folding and rolling, lightly flouring only when necessary and pulling pasta gently to stretch as it comes out of machine, until smooth as suede (*this may take 6 or more rollings*).

Reset rollers for next thinner setting. Lightly flour pasta, but do not fold. Run pasta through machine. Repeat on each thinner setting until as thin as desired. Brush off any excess flour. Repeat with remaining dough. Transfer pasta to towel and let rest until taut but not dry. Cut pasta on noodle or vermicelli setting. Separate strands and allow to dry completely on cloth or cloth-covered pole.

By hand: Divide dough into 8 equal pieces. Roll each piece into as thin a rectangle as desired, using as much flour as necessary. Brush off any excess flour with soft pastry brush. Starting with short end, roll dough up like a jelly roll. Using sharp knife, cut into ¼-inch widths for noodles or 1/16-inch widths for vermicelli. Separate strands and allow to dry completely either on cloth or cloth-covered pole.

To cook: Place pasta in 6 quarts rapidly boiling water to which 2 tablespoons salt have been added. After water returns to boil, cook pasta until al dente, about 30 seconds. Drain well.

Homemade pasta can be frozen.

Basic Semolina Pasta

Semolina gives the resulting pasta firm texture—a "bite"—and a golden color.

Makes about 1 pound

2 cups (about) semolina pasta flour*
3 eggs
4 teaspoons vegetable or olive oil
1 teaspoon salt

All purpose flour

Using food processor fitted with steel knife, mix 1½ cups semolina flour, eggs, oil and salt until dough forms ball. If sticky or wet, add remaining semolina 1 tablespoon at a time, incorporating each completely before adding the next; dough should form ball that moves easily around work bowl. Process 40 seconds to knead. Wrap in plastic. Let stand at room temperature for 30 minutes.

Cut dough into 8 pieces. Flatten 1 piece of dough (keep remainder covered), then fold into thirds and lightly dust with all purpose flour. Turn pasta machine to widest setting. Run dough through until smooth and velvety, folding before each run and dusting with flour if sticky, about 8 times. Adjust pasta machine to next narrower setting. Run dough through machine without folding, dusting with flour if necessary. Repeat, narrowing rollers until dough is 1/16 inch thick. Cut as directed.** Cook within several hours or wrap tightly and refrigerate up to 3 days. (*Pasta can also be dried at room temperature, wrapped airtight and stored up to 2 weeks or frozen up to 3 months.*)

Add pasta to large pot of rapidly boiling salted water, stirring to prevent sticking. Cook until just tender but firm to bite, about 30 seconds for fresh pasta. Drain thoroughly.

*Available at natural foods stores, Italian, Middle Eastern and East Indian markets.

*****Cutting Directions***

For fettuccine: Run dough sheets through fettuccine blades. Separate strands and sprinkle with semolina flour. Dry pasta on towels or rack.

For ravioli circles: Arrange pasta on lightly floured surface. Cut into 3-inch rounds using fluted cutter or glass. Dry rounds in single layer on towels. (Makes about 64 ravioli circles.)

For lasagne noodles: Trim edges of pasta sheets. Cut into 11 × 3½-inch noodles. Dry in single layer on towels. (Makes about 20 lasagne noodles.)

Broccoli Pasta

Roll and cut this delicately flavored pasta into any desired shape, then cook and toss with butter (or olive oil), garlic and freshly grated Parmesan cheese.

Makes about 1½ pounds

1 10-ounce package frozen broccoli

3 cups all purpose flour
2 eggs, room temperature
1 tablespoon olive oil
½ teaspoon salt
Additional all purpose flour

Cook broccoli in saucepan of rapidly boiling water until tender, 4 to 6 minutes. Drain well. Squeeze broccoli to remove liquid; pat dry. Mix broccoli in processor to textured puree.

Arrange flour in mound on work surface or in large bowl and make well in center. Add broccoli, eggs, oil and salt to well and blend with fork. Gradually draw flour from inner edge of well into center until all flour is incorporated. Lightly flour work surface and hands. Knead dough until smooth and elastic, about 10 to 12 minutes, kneading in additional flour as necessary. Cover pasta dough with inverted bowl or cloth and let rest at least 30 minutes before rolling and cutting.

Carrot Pasta

Makes 13 ounces (8 servings)

2 unpeeled medium carrots, trimmed (4 ounces total)
2 quarts boiling water
1 tablespoon salt
1½ cups unbleached all purpose flour *or* 1½ cups instant flour mixed with 2 tablespoons semolina
½ teaspoon salt

1 egg

Cook carrots in boiling water with 1 tablespoon salt until tender. Hold under cold running water until cold to the touch. Drain well and pat as dry as possible with paper towels.

Using food processor fitted with steel knife, chop carrots using 2 on/off turns; then let machine run until carrots are pureed, stopping machine as necessary to scrape down sides of bowl. Add egg and mix 2 seconds. Add remaining ingredients and process until dough forms ball. (Dough should not be wet. Add more flour by the tablespoonful if necessary, processing until dough is smooth, about 40 seconds.) Wrap dough in plastic and let rest 30 minutes.

On well-floured board, divide dough into 8 equal pieces and follow rolling and cooking instructions for Basic Processor Pasta (see page 2).

Pasta (Farinacei)

Pasta is the most complex of all Italian menu categories. There are hundreds of different varieties and, to compound the confusion, the same pasta is often called three or four different names in different parts of Italy. The important thing is that most are made from flour and water—the variations are mainly in form, not in substance.

Some waiters like to make customers feel like they've just landed from Mars by mentioning some arcane pasta and giving the impression that everybody in the country has it for dinner at least twice a week. Pay no attention and don't be intimidated. The waiter is probably Bulgarian by birth.

SPAGHETTI. There are many different thicknesses of this most popular form of pasta. The thinner ones are sometimes called *spaghettini,* an even thinner version is known as *vermicelli,* "little worms," and the thinnest of all are *capellini* or *capelli d'angelo,* "angel's hair."

Another form of spaghetti, in the form of a narrow thick noodle, is the popular *linguine,* "small tongues," which come in several thicknesses.

NOODLES. Among the best-loved are *fettuccine,* "small ribbons," which look just like American egg noodles, and *tagliatelle,* which can be as wide as ¾ of an inch. *Pappardelle* are the broadest of all and sometimes have a scalloped edge.

MACARONI. In Sicily, Naples and other parts of Southern Italy, round hollow pasta is more the rule. The general name for this kind of pasta is *macaroni.* A thick version, called *bucatini* (also known as *perciatelli*), is usually cut into long lengths and is about twice the thickness of standard spaghetti. *Ziti* are tubes that usually are cut into two-inch lengths. *Rigatoni* are larger and longer tubes with grooves, or *rigati,* on the outside.

RAVIOLI AND OTHER STUFFED PASTA. These varieties are stuffed with meat, cheese or a vegetable puree. *Ravioli* are very popular square packets and *agnolotti* are semicircular ravioli. In some parts of Northern Italy ravioli are called *pansotti. Tortellini* are ring-shaped pastas finished with a twist.

One of the easiest kinds of pasta to make is the big flat sheets that are used for *lasagne.* These sheets of pasta can also be wrapped around a stuffing to make *cannelloni* or *manicotti.*

NOVELTY PASTAS. This last category is for all the novelty shapes that have been invented just to delight the eye. Some of the most common of these are: *conchiglie,* "seashells"; *farfalle,* "butterflies" or bows; *fusilli,* "twists" that look like corkscrews; *orzo,* small pasta that looks like grains of rice; *penne,* a form of ziti that has to be cut on the slant to form an end that looks like a pen; *orecchiette,* domed pasta that looks like "little ears"; *rotelle,* little "wheels" complete with spokes; and *stellette,* "stars" used mostly in soups.

The following are often listed on the menu with pasta:

GNOCCHI. Little dumplings, popular since Caesar's time, that can be made either with potatoes or semolina flour. They are baked or served, like pasta, with a sauce.

POLENTA. Cornmeal mush that has been fried or baked and cut into thick slices. In Venice, *polenta* accompanies most main dishes.

RISOTTO MILANESE. In Milan, fat-grained Arborio rice is cooked with chicken broth, onions, saffron and lots of freshly grated Parmesan cheese. Like pasta, risotto is served *al dente* ("to the tooth"), meaning chewy.

Green Pea Farfalle

These little pasta "bow ties" are surprisingly easy to shape.

Makes about 1¾ pounds

- 1 10-ounce package frozen tiny peas
- 1 tablespoon unsalted butter
- 3 cups all purpose flour
- 3 eggs, room temperature
- 1 tablespoon olive oil
- ½ teaspoon salt
- Additional all purpose flour

Cook frozen peas in small saucepan of boiling water until just tender, about 4 to 5 minutes; drain well. Puree in processor. Measure ⅔ cup puree for pasta dough and blend in butter.

Arrange flour in mound on work surface or in large bowl and make well in center. Add puree, eggs, oil and salt to well and blend with fork. Gradually draw flour from inner edge of well into center until all flour is incorporated. Lightly flour work surface and hands. Knead dough until smooth and elastic, about 5 minutes, kneading in additional flour as necessary. Cover pasta dough with inverted bowl or cloth and let rest at least 20 minutes.

For rolling pasta by machine: Cut pasta dough into 4 pieces. Turn pasta machine to widest setting. Flatten 1 piece of dough (keep remainder covered to prevent drying), then fold in half or thirds and run through machine. Repeat until smooth and velvety (number of times will depend on how vigorously dough was kneaded by hand). Adjust pasta machine to next narrower setting. Run dough through machine, dusting lightly with flour if sticky. Repeat, narrowing rollers after each run until pasta is 1/16 inch thick. *Immediately cut and shape bow ties before rolling remaining dough.*

For cutting and shaping bow ties: Using fluted pastry wheel, cut dough into 1 × 2-inch rectangles. Pinch long sides of rectangles together in center to form bow ties. Arrange pasta on kitchen towel, overlapping as little as possible. Repeat rolling and cutting with remaining dough. Set aside until ready to cook.

Lemon Tagliolini

Makes about 1 pound

- 2½ to 3 cups all purpose flour
- 2 eggs, room temperature
- ¼ cup strained fresh lemon juice
- 8 teaspoons minced lemon peel
- 1 to 3 tablespoons warm water
- 1 tablespoon olive oil
- ½ teaspoon salt

Arrange 2½ cups flour in mound on work surface or in large bowl and make well in center. Add eggs, lemon juice, lemon peel, 1 tablespoon water, oil and salt to well and blend with fork. Gradually draw small amount of flour from inner edge of well into center until all flour is incorporated, adding more water if necessary to bind dough. Lightly flour work surface and hands. Knead dough until smooth and elastic, 10 to 12 minutes, kneading in remaining flour as necessary. Cover with inverted bowl or cloth and let rest at least 30 minutes.

For rolling pasta by machine: Roll pasta as for Orange Pappardelle (see next recipe).

For cutting tagliolini: Run dough sheets through narrowest blades of pasta machine. Arrange pasta on kitchen towel or drying rack, overlapping as little as possible. Set aside until ready to cook.

Orange Pappardelle

Makes about 1½ pounds

- **3 cups all purpose flour**
- **3 eggs, room temperature**
- **3 to 4 tablespoons strained fresh orange juice**
- **2 tablespoons minced orange peel**
- **1 tablespoon olive oil**
- **½ teaspoon salt**
- **Additional all purpose flour**

Arrange flour in mound on work surface or in large bowl and make well in center. Add eggs, 3 tablespoons orange juice, orange peel, oil and salt to well and blend with fork. Gradually draw flour from inner edge of well into center until all flour is incorporated, adding remaining juice if necessary to bind dough. Lightly flour work surface and hands. Knead dough until smooth and elastic, about 10 to 12 minutes, kneading in additional flour as necessary. Cover with inverted bowl or cloth; let rest at least 30 minutes.

For rolling pasta by machine: Cut pasta dough into 4 pieces. Turn pasta machine to widest setting. Flatten 1 piece of dough (keep remainder covered to prevent drying), then fold in half or thirds and run through machine. Repeat until smooth and velvety (number of times will depend on how vigorously dough was kneaded by hand). Adjust machine to next narrower setting. Run dough through machine, dusting lightly with flour if sticky. Repeat, narrowing rollers until pasta is 1/16 inch thick. Hang dough sheet on drying rack or set on kitchen towels. Repeat with remaining dough. Dry sheets until firm and leathery and edges begin to curl slightly, but are not brittle, 10 to 30 minutes, depending on moistness of dough and temperature of kitchen. *Pasta must be cut at this point or dough will be too brittle.*

For cutting pappardelle: Cut 1 dough sheet into 5/8-inch-wide ribbons using fluted pastry wheel. Arrange pasta on drying rack or kitchen towel, overlapping as little as possible. Repeat with remaining dough. Set pappardelle aside until ready to cook.

Red Pepper Pasta

Makes about 1 pound

- **1 medium-size red bell pepper (6 ounces), peeled, cored and cut into 2-inch pieces***
- **2 to 2¼ cups unbleached all purpose flour**
- **1 egg**
- **1 teaspoon Hungarian sweet paprika**
- **1 teaspoon salt**

Using food processor fitted with steel knife, place pepper in work bowl and puree 15 seconds. Add 1¾ cups flour, egg, paprika and salt and mix 10 seconds. Blend in remaining flour 1 tablespoon at a time until dough leaves sides of work bowl but is still soft. Process until smooth, about 40 seconds. Wrap dough in plastic. Let rest at room temperature for 30 minutes.

Using pasta machine: Divide dough into 4 equal pieces. Lightly flour 1 piece of dough (wrap remainder in plastic to prevent drying). Set rollers for widest setting. Run dough through rollers once. Flour lightly, fold into thirds and run through rollers again. Repeat folding and rolling dough, lightly flouring only as necessary, until very soft and smooth *(this may take 8 or more times).*

Reset rollers for next setting. Lightly flour dough but do not fold. Run through machine. Repeat on each thinner setting until dough is as thin as desired. Brush off any excess flour. Repeat with remaining pieces of dough.

Dry dough slightly on rack or towels until firm but not brittle. Cut pasta on fettuccine or vermicelli setting. Separate strands and let pasta dry completely on rack or baking sheets.

By hand: Divide dough into 4 equal pieces. Roll each piece into as thin a rectangle as desired, flouring only when necessary. Brush off any excess flour with soft pastry brush. Starting at short end, roll dough up as for jelly roll. Using sharp knife, cut into 1/4-inch widths for fettuccine or 1/16-inch widths for vermicelli. Separate strands and allow to dry completely.

*If fresh red bell peppers are not available, prepare pasta using one 4-ounce jar pimientos (undrained), 2 1/4 cups unbleached all purpose flour, 1 egg, 1/2 teaspoon Hungarian sweet paprika and 1/2 teaspoon salt. Puree pimientos with juice 5 seconds. Add 2 cups flour, egg, paprika and salt and mix 10 seconds, then proceed as above.

Saffron Pasta

Makes about 1 1/4 pounds

3 3/4 cups all purpose flour
1/2 teaspoon salt
4 jumbo eggs
1 teaspoon saffron threads, crushed to powder and dissolved in 1 tablespoon warm water
Additional all purpose flour

Combine 3 3/4 cups flour and salt in large bowl and make well in center. Add eggs and saffron to well and blend with fork. Gradually draw flour from inner edge of well into center until all flour is incorporated. Knead dough on lightly floured surface until smooth, about 5 minutes, kneading in additional flour if necessary. Cover with towel and let rest 30 minutes.

Cut dough into 5 pieces. Flatten 1 piece of dough (keep remainder covered) with heel of hand, then fold in half or thirds. Turn pasta machine to widest setting and run dough through about 10 times or until smooth and velvety (number of times will depend on how vigorously dough was kneaded by hand). Adjust pasta machine to next narrower setting. Run dough through machine, dusting with flour if sticky. Repeat, narrowing rollers after each run until pasta is 1/16 inch thick. Hang dough sheet on drying rack or place on kitchen towels. Repeat with remaining dough. Set aside until sheets look firm and leathery and edges begin to curl but are not brittle, 10 to 30 minutes, depending on dampness of dough and temperature of kitchen. *Pasta must be cut at this point.*

Run dough sheets through fettuccine blades of pasta machine (or cut by hand into 1/4-inch-wide strips). Arrange on kitchen towel or drying rack, overlapping as little as possible. Set aside until ready to cook.

Tomato Basil Pasta

Makes about 1 pound

1 6-ounce can tomato paste
2 eggs, room temperature
2 tablespoons fresh basil leaves or 1 tablespoon dried
2 1/2 cups (about) unbleached all purpose flour
1/2 teaspoon salt

Additional all purpose flour

Using food processor fitted with steel knife, combine tomato paste, eggs and basil in work bowl and mix 3 seconds. Add 2 cups flour and salt and process until dough forms ball. If dough is too wet, add remaining flour 1 tablespoon at a time and blend until dough cleans sides of work bowl. Process until smooth, about 40 seconds. Wrap dough in plastic. Let dough rest at room temperature at least 30 minutes.

Using pasta machine: Divide dough into 4 equal pieces. Set rollers for widest setting. Lightly flour first piece of dough (wrap remainder in plastic to prevent drying). Run through rollers once. Flour lightly, fold into thirds (as for business letter) and run through rollers again. Repeat folding and rolling, lightly flouring dough only as necessary, until dough is very soft and smooth *(this may take 8 or more rollings)*.

Reset rollers for next setting. Lightly flour dough but do not fold. Run through machine. Repeat on each thinner setting until dough is as thin as desired. Brush off any excess flour. Repeat with remaining pieces of dough. Dry dough slightly on rack or towels until firm but not brittle. Cut pasta on fettuccine or vermicelli setting. Separate strands and dry completely on rack.

By hand: Divide dough into 4 equal pieces. Roll each piece into as thin a rectangle as desired, flouring when necessary. Brush off any excess flour with soft pastry brush. Starting at short end, roll dough up as for jelly roll. Using sharp knife, cut into 1/4-inch widths for fettuccine or 1/16-inch widths for vermicelli. Separate strands and allow to dry completely.

Tomato Tagliolini

Makes about 1 1/4 pounds

2 1/2 cups all purpose flour
3 eggs, room temperature
3 tablespoons tomato paste
1 tablespoon olive oil
1/2 teaspoon salt
Additional all purpose flour

Arrange flour in mound on work surface or in large bowl and make well in center. Add eggs, tomato paste, oil and salt to well and blend with fork (tomato paste will not blend completely with eggs, but it will blend into pasta as it is worked). Gradually draw flour from inner edge of well into center until all flour is incorporated. Lightly flour work surface and hands. Knead dough until smooth and elastic, 8 to 10 minutes, kneading in additional flour as necessary. Cover with inverted bowl or cloth; let rest at least 20 minutes.

For rolling pasta by machine: Roll pasta as for Orange Pappardelle (see recipe on page 6).

For cutting tagliolini: Run dough sheets through narrowest blades of pasta machine. Arrange pasta on kitchen towel or drying rack, overlapping as little as possible. Set aside until ready to cook.

Green Onion Pasta

6 servings

6 large green onions, trimmed and cut into-1-inch pieces
1/4 cup fresh parsley leaves
2 eggs
2 1/4 cups (about) unbleached all purpose flour
1/4 cup (1/2 stick) unsalted butter, cut into 4 pieces, room temperature

Using food processor fitted with steel knife, mince green onions and parsley. Add eggs and blend 5 seconds. Add 1 3/4 cups flour and salt and mix just until dough forms ball, about 5 seconds. If dough is sticky, mix in remaining 1/2 cup flour 1 tablespoon at a time. Wrap in plastic and let stand at room temperature 30 minutes.

For rolling pasta by machine: Divide dough into 8 pieces. Lightly flour 1 piece. Wrap remainder in plastic to prevent drying. Set rollers for widest setting. Run 1 piece through rollers once. Flour lightly, fold into thirds and run through rollers again. Repeat folding and rolling dough, lightly flouring only as necessary, until very soft and smooth, about 6 more times. Adjust rollers for next narrower setting. Lightly flour dough and run through machine. Repeat, narrowing rollers until dough is 1/16 inch thick. Brush off any excess flour. Hang dough on drying rack or set on towels. Repeat with remaining pieces. Dry until firm but not brittle, 10 to 30 minutes, depending on moistness of dough and temperature of kitchen. Run dough through fettuccine or vermicelli blades. Separate strands of pasta and dry completely on rack or towels.

For rolling pasta by hand: Divide dough into 8 pieces. Roll each into rectangle 1/16 inch thick, lightly flouring as necessary. Brush off excess flour. Starting at short end, roll dough up as for jelly roll. Using sharp knife, cut into 1/4-inch widths for fettuccine or 1/16-inch widths for vermicelli. Separate strands and dry on rack or towels.

Add pasta to large amount of rapidly boiling salted water in stockpot, stirring to prevent sticking. Cook until just firm but tender to the bite (al dente), about 30 seconds. Drain well. Toss with butter. Serve immediately.

Mrs. Sinatra's Gnocchi Verdi

6 to 8 servings

6 tablespoons (3/4 stick) butter
3 10-ounce packages frozen chopped spinach, thawed, squeezed dry and minced
1 cup plus 2 tablespoons ricotta cheese
6 tablespoons freshly grated Parmesan cheese
1/2 cup plus 1 tablespoon all purpose flour
3 eggs, well beaten
3/4 teaspoon salt
Freshly ground pepper

Melted butter
3/4 cup freshly grated Parmesan cheese

Additional freshly grated Parmesan cheese (optional)

Melt butter in heavy large skillet over medium heat. Add spinach and sauté until all moisture has evaporated. Add ricotta and continue cooking several minutes, stirring constantly. Turn into large bowl. Add 6 tablespoons Parmesan, flour, eggs, salt and pepper and blend well. Cover and refrigerate until firm enough to handle, about 1 hour.

Bring 4 quarts salted water to rapid boil in large saucepan or Dutch oven. Dust hands with flour. Shape mixture into balls no larger than 1 1/2 inches in diameter. Reduce heat to medium, add gnocchi in batches and simmer until expanded slightly and firm but light, about 6 to 8 minutes. Remove with slotted spoon and drain on non-terry towel. Divide gnocchi evenly among soup bowls, drizzle with butter and sprinkle with remaining cheese. Pass additional Parmesan separately if desired. Serve immediately.

Pumpkin Gnocchi with Walnut Cream Sauce

Adapted from a specialty of Al Tartufo in Salsomaggiore, Italy.

4 to 6 first-course servings

2 pounds pumpkin or winter squash (acorn or hubbard), halved vertically
10 to 11 ounces russet potatoes

1 teaspoon salt
1/8 teaspoon freshly ground pepper
1/8 teaspoon freshly grated nutmeg
14 to 20 tablespoons all purpose flour

1½ cups whipping cream
½ cup coarsely chopped toasted walnuts
Salt and freshly ground pepper
Freshly grated nutmeg
½ cup freshly grated Parmesan cheese
Parsley or chervil sprigs
Additional freshly grated Parmesan cheese (optional)

Preheat oven to 350°F. Arrange pumpkin halves cut side down with potatoes in large glass baking dish. Bake until both are very tender and easily pierced with tip of sharp knife, about 1 hour.

Remove and discard pumpkin skin and seeds. Peel potatoes. Press pumpkin pulp through fine sieve with mallet (scraping bottom of sieve) into heavy large saucepan. Repeat with potato pulp. Cook over low heat until mixture masses together and is very dry, stirring frequently with wooden spoon, 20 to 25 minutes. Stir in salt, pepper and nutmeg. Remove from heat and blend in 14 tablespoons flour, adding as much of remaining flour as necessary to make smooth, manageable yet slightly sticky dough.

Lightly flour baking sheet. Shape dough into several ¾-inch-wide cylinders on lightly floured surface. Cut cylinders into rounds ¼ inch thick. Press top of each round lightly with floured fork. Make indentation in center of each round with floured fork handle, curling dough round up around handle. Transfer gnocchi to prepared sheet. *(Can be prepared 1 day ahead. Cover with plastic wrap and refrigerate.)*

Bring large pot of salted water to boil. Add gnocchi in batches. After each batch rises to surface, cook 3 minutes. Transfer to colander with slotted spoon. *(Can be prepared several hours ahead. Store at room temperature.)*

Combine gnocchi, cream, walnuts, salt, pepper and nutmeg in large, shallow, flameproof baking dish. Bring to simmer over medium heat and cook until cream thickens to saucelike consistency. Sprinkle with ½ cup Parmesan. Remove from heat and let stand 5 minutes. Garnish with parsley or chervil and serve. Pass additional grated Parmesan cheese if desired.

2 *Pasta with Butter, Cheese and Cream Sauces*

In this chapter you will find some of the simplest and most classic of all pasta sauces. While these cheese, butter and cream mixtures are rich and satisfying, most are assembled in minutes—a definite plus for busy contemporary cooks.

All of the recipes are suitable for purchased dried pasta, and some are particularly appropriate for homemade noodles as well: Linguine with Freshly Grated Nutmeg and Pepper (page 12), Easy Fettuccine (page 14) and the creamy Gorgonzola and mascarpone sauces on pages 15 to 16 are all perfect for showing off plain or flavored homemade pasta to its best advantage.

If these rich dishes are served as a first course, keep the entrée simple and light. Quickly sautéed chicken, veal or fish fillets would be excellent, needing only a tossed salad and perhaps a loaf of crusty bread to round out the meal. If the pasta is to be the main dish, start with an antipasto platter of crisp fresh and marinated vegetables, and finish off with fresh fruit or a fruit-based dessert. In either case you will have an elegant but fast-to-fix meal.

Linguine with Freshly Grated Nutmeg and Pepper

4 servings

- 1 pound linguine, freshly cooked and drained
- 2/3 cup unsalted butter, room temperature
- Freshly grated nutmeg
- Freshly ground pepper
- Freshly grated Parmesan cheese (garnish)

Combine linguine and butter in large bowl and toss until thoroughly coated. Transfer to serving platter. Sprinkle nutmeg and pepper over top and toss well. Garnish with Parmesan cheese and serve immediately.

New Orleans Peppered Butter Sauce

This spicy butter can also be brushed on barbecued prawns, grilled beef, French bread or boiled potatoes.

Makes 2 cups

- 1 cup (2 sticks) butter
- 1 cup olive oil
- 2 tablespoons dry Sherry
- 1 tablespoon fresh lemon juice
- 1 tablespoon minced fresh rosemary leaves or 1 teaspoon dried, crumbled
- 1 tablespoon minced fresh parsley
- 3 garlic cloves, minced
- 1 teaspoon Hungarian sweet paprika
- 1 teaspoon dried oregano, crumbled
- 1 teaspoon dried basil, crumbled
- 3/4 teaspoon coarsely ground pepper
- 1/2 teaspoon ground red pepper
- 1/4 teaspoon hot pepper sauce
- Freshly cooked pasta

Melt butter in heavy medium saucepan over medium heat. Stir in remaining ingredients and cook just until sauce comes to boil. Reduce heat to medium-low and cook 10 minutes, stirring occasionally. Let cool. Refrigerate for 6 hours, then toss with hot pasta just before serving.

Pasta Pilaf

8 servings

- 1/4 cup (1/2 stick) unsalted butter
- 1 medium onion, chopped
- 1 medium garlic clove, crushed
- 2 cups orzo (rice-shaped pasta)
- 2 1/2 cups chicken stock, heated to boiling
- 1/2 cup grated Gruyère or Fontina cheese

Melt butter in heavy large skillet over low heat. Add onion and garlic, cover and cook until onion is translucent, about 10 minutes. Discard garlic. Stir in orzo. Pour in hot stock. Cover and remove from heat. Let stand until liquid is absorbed, about 25 minutes. Stir in cheese until melted. Serve hot.

Paglia e Fieno (Straw and Hay)

6 servings

- 8 ounces thin green noodles (about 1/8 inch wide)
- 8 ounces thin noodles (about 1/8 inch wide)
- 1/2 cup (1 stick) butter
- 4 ounces prosciutto, minced
- 1 10-ounce package frozen tiny peas, thawed
- 1 cup half and half
- 1/2 lightly beaten egg yolk
- 1 cup freshly grated Parmesan cheese
- Pinch of freshly grated nutmeg

Generously butter 2-quart rectangular baking dish. Add noodles to large pot of rapidly boiling salted water. Return to boil and cook until al dente. Drain well. Transfer to prepared baking dish.

Preheat oven to 400°F. Melt butter in medium saucepan over medium-high heat. Add prosciutto and sauté 2 to 3 minutes. Reduce heat, stir in peas, half and half, egg yolk, 3/4 cup Parmesan and nutmeg and blend well. Pour over noodles and toss. Sprinkle with remaining cheese. Bake until top is golden, about 8 to 10 minutes. Serve immediately.

Creamy Spinach Noodles

4 to 6 servings

6 tablespoons (3/4 stick) unsalted butter
1 cup sliced mushrooms
1/4 cup all purpose flour
1 cup milk
1 cup whipping cream
1 teaspoon salt
8 ounces spinach noodles, freshly cooked and drained
Freshly grated Parmesan cheese

Melt 2 tablespoons butter in small skillet over low heat. Increase heat to medium-high. Add mushrooms and sauté until tender, about 4 minutes. Remove from heat and set aside.

Melt remaining butter in 3-quart saucepan over medium heat. Remove from heat. Blend in flour. Return to medium heat and cook, stirring constantly, for 2 to 3 minutes. Remove from heat. Stir in milk, cream and salt. Cook, stirring constantly, until thickened, about 5 minutes. Stir in mushrooms. Transfer to large bowl. Add noodles and toss well. Garnish with Parmesan cheese.

For a sharper taste, 1/4 to 1/2 cup grated asiago cheese may be added to the cream sauce before tossing pasta.

Pasta Allegra

4 main-course servings

1 ounce dried porcini* *or* 1 cup sliced, sautéed mushrooms
1 cup hot water
3 cups whipping cream
1/2 cup (1 stick) unsalted butter
1/4 cup minced shallot
1 teaspoon minced garlic
1/3 cup slivered almonds
1/2 cup minced fresh parsley
2 tablespoons Cognac
1/4 teaspoon freshly grated nutmeg
1/4 teaspoon freshly ground white pepper
Salt
3/4 cup freshly grated Parmesan cheese
1 pound spinach fettuccine, cooked al dente

Soak porcini in 1 cup hot water until soft, about 15 minutes. Squeeze porcini dry, discard any hard pieces and slice. Boil cream in large saucepan over medium-high heat until reduced to 2 cups, about 10 minutes. Set aside. Melt butter in small skillet over low heat. Sauté shallot and garlic until very soft, about 15 minutes. Add almonds and sauté until golden, 2 to 3 minutes. Add shallot mixture to reduced cream. Stir in porcini, parsley, Cognac, nutmeg, pepper and salt. Add cheese and blend well. Pour over hot pasta and toss. Serve immediately.

*Porcini (dried mushrooms) are available at Italian markets.

Zelda's Fettuccine

6 servings

- 2 cups sour cream
- 3/4 cup freshly grated Parmesan cheese
- 1/4 cup dry vermouth
- 1 tablespoon all purpose flour
- 1 tablespoon fresh lemon juice
- 2 garlic cloves, pressed
- 1/2 teaspoon (scant) oregano, crumbled
- 1/2 teaspoon (scant) basil, crumbled
- 1/2 teaspoon dried marjoram, crumbled
- Salt and freshly ground pepper
- 1/2 cup (1 stick) butter
- 12 ounces fettuccine or spinach noodles, freshly cooked and drained

Combine first 11 ingredients in medium bowl and blend thoroughly. Melt butter in medium saucepan over low heat. Stir in sour cream mixture and simmer 20 minutes. Combine sauce and cooked fettuccine or spinach noodles in large bowl and toss thoroughly. Serve immediately.

Garden Sauce with Cottage Cheese

4 servings

- 2 cups small-curd cottage cheese
- 1 bunch watercress, washed, stemmed and coarsely chopped
- 2 cucumbers, peeled, seeded and coarsely chopped
- 3 green onions, finely chopped
- Salt and freshly ground pepper to taste
- 1 pound pasta, freshly cooked and drained

Combine cottage cheese, watercress, cucumber, onion, salt and pepper in large bowl and mix well. Add pasta and toss to coat. Serve immediately.

Easy Fettuccine

4 main-course or 6 side-dish servings

- 1/4 cup (1/2 stick) butter or margarine, room temperature
- 2 tablespoons chopped fresh parsley
- 1 teaspoon dried basil, crumbled
- 1 8-ounce package cream cheese, room temperature
- Freshly ground pepper
- 2/3 cup boiling water
- 1/4 cup (1/2 stick) butter or margarine
- 1 garlic clove, minced
- 8 ounces fettuccine, freshly cooked and drained
- 3/4 cup freshly grated Romano cheese

Combine 1/4 cup butter, parsley and basil in medium bowl. Blend in cream cheese. Season with pepper. Mix in water, blending thoroughly. Set bowl in larger pan of hot water to keep warm.

Melt remaining butter in large skillet over low heat. Add garlic and cook about 1 to 2 minutes; do not burn. Add pasta and toss gently. Sprinkle with 1/2 cup cheese and toss again. Transfer to serving platter. Spoon sauce over top and sprinkle with remaining cheese. Serve immediately.

Pasta with Gorgonzola Sauce

4 servings

8 ounces Gorgonzola cheese, crumbled
1 cup crème fraîche

1 pound pasta, freshly cooked and drained

1 avocado, peeled, pitted and thinly sliced
Freshly ground pepper

Mix cheese and crème fraîche in medium bowl until smooth or combine in medium saucepan over low heat and stir until cheese melts.

Place pasta in shallow large serving bowl and pour sauce over. Add avocado and pepper, toss gently and serve.

Fettuccine au Gorgonzola

4 first-course servings

6 ounces thin julienne of combined carrot, celery and turnip

2 cups whipping cream
1 ounce Parmesan cheese, freshly grated
1 ounce Gruyère cheese, grated
1 garlic clove, chopped
Salt and freshly ground pepper

8 ounces fettuccine
2 tablespoons olive oil

3 ounces Gorgonzola cheese, diced
Chopped fresh parsley (garnish)

Steam vegetable julienne in medium saucepan over medium-high heat until just crisp-tender. Rinse under cold running water and drain.

Simmer whipping cream in large saucepan over medium-high heat for 10 minutes. Reduce heat to low, add Parmesan, Gruyère, garlic, salt and pepper and blend well. Continue cooking 10 minutes, stirring frequently to prevent bottom from scorching.

Meanwhile, cook fettuccine in large amount of boiling water with 2 tablespoons olive oil until al dente.

Blend vegetable julienne into sauce. Drain fettuccine well. Add to sauce. Blend in Gorgonzola and mix 3 minutes. Turn into dish, sprinkle with chopped parsley and serve.

Fettuccine with Gorgonzola Cream Sauce

The fresh herbs in this quick and easy pasta dish can be varied according to what is available.

4 servings

4 tablespoons (1/2 stick) butter
1 small onion, chopped
2 cups whipping cream
10 fresh sage leaves, cut into julienne
1 cup crumbled Gorgonzola cheese
Salt and freshly ground pepper

1 pound fresh fettuccine or spaghetti
2 tablespoons toasted pine nuts
Minced fresh parsley

Melt 2 tablespoons butter in heavy medium saucepan over low heat. Add onion and cook until translucent, stirring frequently, about 8 minutes. Mix in cream and sage. Bring to boil, reduce heat and simmer until sauce thickens slightly, about 5 minutes. Add cheese and stir until smooth. Season sauce with salt and freshly ground pepper.

Meanwhile, cook pasta in large pot of boiling salted water until just tender but firm to bite. Drain well and transfer to heated platter. Cut remaining 2 tablespoons butter into small pieces and stir into sauce until melted. Pour over pasta and toss to combine. Sprinkle with nuts and parsley and serve.

Pasta with Mascarpone Sauce

6 servings

2 tablespoons (1/4 stick) butter
1 medium onion, finely chopped
8 ounces cream cheese
4 ounces mascarpone cheese (substitute Gorgonzola cheese if mascarpone is unavailable)
4 cups whipping cream
Salt and freshly ground white pepper

12 to 16 ounces fettuccine, freshly cooked and drained

Melt butter in 3-quart saucepan over medium-low heat. Add onion and sauté until golden brown, about 10 minutes. Whisk in cheeses, blending until mixture is smooth. Remove from heat and set aside.

Bring whipping cream to boil in large saucepan over high heat. Remove from heat. Place cheese mixture over medium-high heat. Gradually whisk in hot cream and bring mixture to slow boil. Let boil 4 to 5 minutes, whisking constantly, until thickened and reduced by about half. Season with salt and freshly ground white pepper.

Combine fettuccine and sauce in large serving bowl and toss to coat pasta well. Serve immediately.

Ravioli al Burro

4 servings

Pasta
3 egg yolks
1 egg
2 tablespoons water
1 teaspoon olive oil
1/2 teaspoon salt
1 3/4 cups all purpose flour

Filling
8 ounces ricotta cheese
2 ounces cream cheese, room temperature
1 pound Swiss chard (leaves only) or spinach, cooked, squeezed dry and finely chopped
Pinch *each* of salt and freshly ground pepper
2 eggs
2 cups freshly grated Parmesan cheese

Melted butter
Minced garlic
Freshly grated Parmesan cheese (garnish)

For pasta: Combine egg yolks, egg, water, oil and salt in medium bowl and mix thoroughly. Spoon 1 1/2 cups flour into large bowl. Make well in center and add egg mixture. Stir with fork until flour is moistened and well mixed. Pat into ball.

Sprinkle remaining 1/4 cup flour onto work surface. Knead dough until smooth and elastic, about 5 to 10 minutes (if using pasta machine, kneading time will be less). Wrap in plastic and refrigerate until ready to use.

For filling: Combine ricotta cheese, cream cheese, Swiss chard, salt and pepper in large bowl. Add eggs and 2 cups Parmesan and blend well. Set aside.

To assemble, flour work surface. Divide pasta in half. Roll one half into thin large rectangle. Drop filling onto pasta by teaspoons, spacing 2 to 2 1/2 inches apart. Dip pastry brush in water and moisten all areas around filling. Roll remaining dough out into thin large rectangle. Position over filled sheet. Press together gently with fingertips, sealing firmly at edges and between filling mounds. Cut into individual squares using ravioli cutter or small sharp knife.

Drop ravioli into boiling water. Cook 6 to 8 minutes. Drain well. Transfer ravioli to platter. Combine butter and garlic to taste and pour over top. Garnish with Parmesan cheese and serve immediately.

Tomato-meat sauce can be substituted for butter-garlic mixture.

Pasta Ramekins with Goat Cheese

6 servings

Pasta Ramekins
1½ cups all purpose flour
2 extra-large eggs, room temperature

Goat Cheese Filling
1 pound goat cheese
½ cup whipping cream
2 eggs
3 sun-dried tomatoes (optional), diced

¼ cup (½ stick) butter, melted (for ramekins and tops of pasta molds)
½ cup freshly grated Parmesan cheese
12 Garlic Croutons* (garnish)

For pasta: Mix flour and eggs in processor 30 seconds; do not let dough form ball (dough should appear moist and hold together when pinched). Divide dough in half. Knead 1 piece slightly in hand to form even ball; flatten slightly. Adjust pasta machine to widest setting. Run dough through machine 5 or 6 times to knead, folding dough in thirds (as for business letter) after each run. Wrap tightly in plastic. Repeat with remaining piece of dough. Let dough rest 15 minutes.

Adjust machine to next narrower setting. Run dough repeatedly through machine (do not fold), adjusting to next narrower setting after each run until dough is about 1/16 inch thick. Cut pasta into six 5-inch circles and six 3½-inch circles. Set aside.

For filling: Combine cheese and cream in large bowl until well blended; cheese should retain some texture. Mix in eggs and tomatoes.

To assemble, position rack in center of oven and preheat to 350°F. Butter six 5-ounce ramekins. Dust with Parmesan, shaking out excess. Bring large amount of salted water to rapid boil. Add pasta and cook until just tender to the bite (al dente), about 2 minutes (cooking time will depend on dryness of pasta). Drain well. Line ramekins with larger pasta circles. Add cheese mixture, filling molds ¾ full. Set smaller circles on top. Brush well with butter and sprinkle with Parmesan. Bake until molds are puffed and tops are brown and slightly crusty, 20 to 25 minutes. Transfer to individual plates.

Unmold if desired. Garnish each with 2 croutons. Serve immediately.

*Garlic Croutons

Makes 12

12 ½-inch-thick slices French bread from narrow baguette
6 tablespoons olive oil
1 garlic clove, halved

Preheat oven to 400°F. Brush both sides of bread slices with oil. Transfer to baking sheet. Bake until evenly browned, about 10 minutes per side. Very gently rub top of crouton with cut side of garlic to flavor lightly.

Green and White Lasagne (Lasagne Verdi e Bianchi)

A hearty dish that can be prepared with or without meat and doubled for a large group. The lasagne can be assembled without the sauce and refrigerated up to three days or frozen up to two months. Pour sauce over top before baking. The sauce can be prepared three days ahead and refrigerated.

10 servings

Herbed Tomato Béchamel Sauce

- 1/4 cup (1/2 stick) butter
- 1/4 cup all purpose flour
- 3 tablespoons chopped fresh basil or 1 tablespoon dried, crumbled
- 3/4 teaspoon fresh thyme or 1/8 teaspoon dried, crumbled
- Generous pinch of dried oregano
- 2 cups milk or half and half
- 1 cup thick tomato puree
- 3 egg yolks
- Salt and freshly ground pepper
- Freshly grated nutmeg
- 1 tablespoon butter, room temperature

Lasagne

- 1/4 cup (1/2 stick) butter
- 2 medium onions, finely chopped
- 3 garlic cloves, minced
- 1/2 cup pine nuts or chopped almonds
- 3 pounds fresh spinach, cooked until wilted, squeezed dry and finely chopped, or five 10-ounce packages frozen spinach, thawed, squeezed dry and finely chopped
- Salt and freshly ground pepper
- Freshly grated nutmeg
- 1/3 cup raisins

- 1 15- to 16-ounce container ricotta cheese
- 8 ounces spicy Italian salami, minced (optional)
- 4 green onions, minced
- 1 egg yolk
- 3 tablespoons minced fresh parsley
- 3 tablespoons fresh basil or 1 tablespoon dried, crumbled
- Salt and freshly ground pepper
- 8 ounces Fontinella cheese, shredded
- 8 ounces Asiago or Parmesan cheese, freshly grated
- 3 ounces Gruyère or Swiss cheese, shredded
- 8 to 12 ounces lasagne noodles, cooked al dente, rinsed and drained on paper towels

For sauce: Melt 1/4 cup butter in heavy nonaluminum saucepan over medium-low heat until bubbly. Remove from heat and whisk in flour, basil, thyme and oregano. Cook, stirring constantly, about 3 to 5 minutes (be careful not to let flour brown). Gradually whisk in milk. Increase heat slightly and cook, stirring constantly, until sauce has thickened. Stir in tomato puree. Remove from heat and let cool about 5 minutes. Whisk in egg yolks. Season with salt, pepper and nutmeg to taste. Transfer to storage container. Spread 1 tablespoon butter over sauce to prevent skin from forming. Cover and refrigerate until ready to use.

For lasagne: Melt butter in large nonaluminum skillet over medium heat. Add onion and cook, stirring frequently, until browned and caramelized, about 25 to 30 minutes. Stir in garlic and nuts and cook about 30 seconds. Mix in spinach and cook, stirring frequently, until dry. Remove from heat and season with salt, pepper and nutmeg to taste. Blend in raisins. Set aside and let cool.

Combine ricotta, salami, green onion, egg yolk, parsley, basil and salt and pepper in medium bowl and blend well. Mix Fontinella, Asiago and Gruyère cheeses in another medium bowl; reserve 1 1/4 cups for topping.

Preheat oven to 375°F. Generously butter 9 × 13-inch baking dish or 2 medium baking dishes. Whisk through chilled sauce several times to lighten. Spread thin layer over bottom of prepared dish(es). Cover with layer of pasta. Top with thin layer of spinach. Dot with ricotta mixture and sprinkle with Fontinella mixture. Repeat layering, ending with pasta. Pour remaining sauce over lasagne and sprinkle with reserved cheeses. Bake until bubbly and lightly browned, about 45 to 60 minutes. Turn off heat; let lasagne stand in oven 20 minutes before cutting into squares and serving.

For variation, spread each lasagne noodle with thin layers of spinach and ricotta mixture. Roll each noodle up jelly roll fashion, tucking small stalk of

Tips and Techniques

- The fresher, moister and thinner the pasta, the shorter the cooking time. Freshly made pasta usually needs only 5 to 20 seconds.
- Pasta stuffed with spinach and cheese should not be prepared more than one day ahead. Refrigerate covered with a kitchen towel.
- Humidity and size of eggs you use will influence amount of flour required to make pasta. Be flexible and make adjustments according to conditions.
- When rolling out pasta dough, be sure to roll over the edges as they are likely to be thicker than the middle.
- If sauce is too thin, thicken by boiling it uncovered until it reaches desired consistency. This will also intensify the flavor of the sauce.
- Pancetta can be cut into pieces and frozen. Bacon can be substituted.

lightly steamed broccoli into each roll. Arrange in bottom of buttered baking dish. Sprinkle with Fontinella mixture. Cover and freeze or refrigerate. Pour sauce over pasta rolls just before baking.

Pasta Timbale with Chianti Vinaigrette

This showstopper can be assembled the night before, baked in the morning and then served at room temperature in the afternoon or evening.

8 to 10 servings

4 large or 8 small leeks, trimmed

1/4 cup olive oil
4 ounces mushrooms, finely chopped
2 garlic cloves, chopped
4 large tomatoes (about 1 1/3 pounds), seeded and chopped
1/4 cup all purpose flour
1 5 1/2-ounce jar oil-cured Greek olives, pitted and coarsely chopped
1/3 cup capers, rinsed and drained
Salt

1 1/2 pounds mozzarella cheese, shredded (6 to 7 cups)

1/2 teaspoon dried oregano, crumbled
18 jumbo round cheese ravioli

8 ounces mortadella, thinly sliced (about 15 slices)

Chianti Vinaigrette
1/3 cup Chianti
1/4 cup red wine vinegar
1 cup olive oil
2 tablespoons minced fresh basil leaves
2 teaspoons salt
1 teaspoon sugar
1/4 teaspoon freshly ground pepper

Generously grease 8-inch springform pan. Cut white part of leeks into 1/4-inch slices. Bring large amount of salted water to rapid boil. Add leek slices and green leaves and simmer 5 minutes. Drain well. Arrange slices in single layer in bottom of springform.Cover with layer of leaves. Drape remaining leaves around sides of springform, allowing ends to hang over top.

Heat olive oil in heavy large saucepan over medium-high heat. Add mushrooms and garlic and sauté 5 minutes. Add tomatoes. Sprinkle vegetables with flour and blend well. Simmer, stirring occasionally, until sauce is thick, about 20 minutes. Stir in olives and capers. Season with salt. Set aside.

Combine cheese and oregano. Bring large amount of salted water to rapid boil. Add ravioli and cook 10 minutes, stirring frequently. Drain and rinse under cold water. Drain and pat day.

Preheat oven to 350°F. Sprinkle 1½ cups cheese mixture over bottom of springform. Layer ⅓ of mortadella slices (about 5) over cheese. Arrange 6 ravioli over top. Pour ⅓ of vegetable sauce over ravioli. Repeat layering, ending with cheese. Fold leek ends over top, pressing gently to flatten layers. Set springform on baking sheet. Cover top of pan with foil. Bake 1 hour. Cool in pan 30 minutes.

For vinaigrette: Mix wine and vinegar in small bowl. Whisk in oil 1 drop at a time. Add basil, salt, sugar and pepper.

To serve, arrange platter over top of springform and invert mold. Carefully remove sides of pan, then gently lift off bottom. Cut timbale into wedges. Pass Chianti vinaigrette separately.

3 *Pasta with Vegetables and Herbs*

Pasta is the perfect foil for the sprightly flavors and colors of fresh vegetables and herbs. This chapter includes vegetable combinations of every conceivable kind, from simple uncooked tomato sauce to luxurious mixtures enriched with cream, butter or olive oil. You will find no less than a half dozen different pesto sauces: In addition to the simple, ever-popular basil pesto there are pimiento, pistachio, spinach, tomato and walnut versions.

When time is short or fresh produce isn't at its peak, you can also whip up splendid pasta dishes using canned or frozen vegetables and other pantryshelf staples. Several recipes, for instance, use black olives to striking effect; others add frozen broccoli, peas or spinach for color and texture. For the ultimate in seasonless simplicity, try the novel *Pasta alla Briciolata* (page 22), consisting of nothing more than garlic-scented breadcrumbs, sautéed in olive oil until golden, tossed with pasta and sprinkled with fresh parsley.

These vegetable and herb combinations are fine counterparts to either homemade or purchased pasta. Experiment with flavored pastas and complementary sauces, letting color as well as taste be your guide. The dishes are guaranteed to bring Mediterranean sunshine to your table, summer and winter alike.

Pasta with Breadcrumb Sauce (Pasta alla Briciolata)

4 to 6 servings

4 quarts water
1 cup plus 2 tablespoons olive oil
Salt
1 pound durum wheat pasta
2 garlic cloves, chopped
3/4 to 1 cup breadcrumbs (preferably homemade)
Chopped fresh parsley (garnish)

Combine water, 1 tablespoon olive oil and 1 heaping tablespoon salt in large saucepan and bring to rapid boil over high heat. Add pasta, stirring once or twice to prevent sticking. While pasta is cooking, heat 1 tablespoon olive oil in medium skillet over high heat. Add garlic and sauté until golden brown; *do not burn.* Remove garlic and set aside. Add remaining 1 cup olive oil and breadcrumbs to same skillet. Reduce heat to medium-high and cook, stirring frequently, until crumbs are golden brown. Remove from heat. Stir in garlic and salt to taste. When pasta is cooked but still firm (al dente), immediately pour 1 cup cold water into saucepan to stop cooking process. Drain pasta in colander. Transfer to heated large bowl. Pour breadcrumb sauce over top and toss well. Sprinkle with chopped parsley. Serve immediately.

Fusilli with Salsa Piccante

This simple sauce welcomes the addition of olives, finely chopped raw or cooked vegetables or julienne of cooked meat. When adding several extras, be sure to increase amounts of oil and vinegar proportionately.

4 servings

1/2 cup olive oil
1/4 cup red wine vinegar *or* dry red wine
1/4 cup tomato puree
3 hard-cooked eggs, finely chopped
2 green onions, finely chopped
1 garlic clove, minced
2 tablespoons minced fresh parsley
Salt and freshly ground pepper

1 pound fusilli, freshly cooked and drained

Combine oil and vinegar in medium bowl. Add tomato puree and mix well. Whisk in egg, onion, garlic, parsley and salt and pepper, blending thoroughly. Let sauce stand at room temperature for at least 1 hour.

Combine fusilli and sauce in shallow large serving bowl. Toss well and serve.

Salsa Verde

4 servings

1 large bunch parsley, stemmed, washed and well drained
2 slices white bread, soaked in water and squeezed dry
2 to 3 anchovy fillets (optional)
3 tablespoons chopped sweet pickle
2 garlic cloves
1 green onion, cut up
1 teaspoon capers, rinsed and drained
1/2 cup olive oil
Salt and freshly ground pepper

1 pound pasta, freshly cooked and drained

Combine parsley, bread, anchovies, sweet pickle, garlic, onion and capers in processor or blender and puree. With machine running, gradually add oil through feed tube in slow steady stream until mixture is consistency of mayonnaise. Add salt and pepper. Let stand at room temperature 2 to 3 hours.

Combine pasta and sauce in shallow large serving bowl, toss well and serve.

Pesto Sauce

4 servings

2 cups firmly packed fresh basil leaves
3/4 cup freshly grated Parmesan cheese
1/4 cup pine nuts
4 garlic cloves
1/2 cup olive oil (about)
1 pound pasta, freshly cooked and drained

Combine basil, cheese, pine nuts and garlic in processor or blender and puree. With machine running, gradually add oil through feed tube in slow steady stream until mixture is consistency of thick mayonnaise. Combine pasta and sauce in shallow large serving bowl and toss well. Serve immediately.

Pesto with Pimientos

6 servings

2 large garlic cloves
3 ounces Parmesan cheese, room temperature, cut into 1-inch cubes
2 cups firmly packed fresh basil leaves, *or* 2 cups Italian parsley leaves or spinach leaves mixed with 2 tablespoons dried basil
1/4 cup pine nuts or walnuts
2 1/2 teaspoons salt
3/4 to 1 cup oil (1 to 3 ratio olive oil and safflower, or other oil of your choice)
1 4-ounce jar pimientos, drained and cut into 1/4-inch dice

Basic Processor Pasta (see page 2)
1 tablespoon olive oil

Using food processor fitted with steel knife, mince garlic by dropping through feed tube with machine running. Add cheese and chop with 10 on/off turns. Add basil leaves, nuts and salt and mince using 8 on/off turns. With machine running, gradually add oil through feed tube, blending thoroughly. Transfer sauce to mixing bowl and fold in diced pimiento.

Cook pasta until al dente; drain well. Transfer to large bowl, add olive oil and toss well. Add pesto and toss again.

Pesto can be refrigerated several months. Top with thin coat of oil before storing. It also freezes very well. Freeze in single servings by dividing among ice cube trays.

Pistachio Pesto

Perfect for pasta, this unique pesto is also excellent on toasted French bread, on sliced tomatoes or in a green bean salad.

Makes 1 1/2 cups

2 large garlic cloves
1/2 teaspoon salt
1 1/2 × 2-inch lemon peel strip, cut into small pieces
2/3 cup natural roasted pistachio nuts, shelled
1 cup fresh basil leaves
1/2 cup fresh parsley leaves
1/2 cup fresh Italian parsley leaves
3/4 cup olive oil
1 tablespoon fresh lemon juice
Olive oil

Mix garlic, salt and lemon peel in processor to very fine paste, about 30 seconds. Blend in pistachios using several on/off turns until very finely ground. Add basil and parsley and blend thoroughly, scraping down sides of bowl frequently. With machine running, slowly add 3/4 cup olive oil and mix until creamy. Blend in lemon juice. Transfer to jar. Cover with thin layer of olive oil; seal tightly. Refrigerate until ready to use. *(Can be prepared 2 weeks ahead.)* Bring pesto to room temperature before serving.

Spinach Pesto

4 servings

- 3 cups fresh spinach leaves, stems discarded
- 2 cups fresh parsley leaves (preferably Italian flat-leaf)
- 1/2 cup freshly grated Parmesan cheese
- 1/2 cup freshly grated Romano cheese
- 1/2 cup vegetable oil
- 1/4 cup blanched almonds
- 1/4 cup (1/2 stick) butter or margarine, melted
- 2 tablespoons pine nuts
- 3 large garlic cloves, crushed
- 1 teaspoon salt

- 1 teaspoon vegetable oil
- Salt
- 1 pound pasta
- Freshly grated Parmesan cheese

Puree first 10 ingredients in blender or processor until smooth; set aside.

Bring water to boil in large pot. Add oil and salt. Add pasta and cook over medium-high heat until al dente. Strain through colander, reserving 1/3 cup liquid. Blend hot liquid into puree and toss with pasta. Serve with Parmesan cheese.

Tomato Pesto with Garlic and Pimiento

A pungent and colorful complement to pasta, fish or chicken.

Makes about 3 cups

- 5 Italian plum tomatoes

- 3 garlic cloves
- 1 teaspoon salt
- 2/3 cup toasted blanched almonds
- 4 large roasted red peppers packed in brine, drained
- 1/8 teaspoon ground red pepper
- 1 cup olive oil
- 3 tablespoons red wine vinegar or 2 tablespoons balsamic vinegar

Char tomatoes in broiler or over flame, turning until skins blacken. Peel off skins. Cut tomatoes in half and squeeze to extract seeds and juice. Drain cut side down on paper towels.

Mix garlic and salt in processor using several on/off turns. Add almonds and grind finely. Blend in peppers using several on/off turns. Add tomatoes and ground red pepper and mix until smooth. With machine running, add oil through feed tube in thin stream. Blend in vinegar. Transfer to bowl. Cover and refrigerate several hours or overnight. Serve at room temperature.

Ligurian Walnut Pesto

If you use young oregano, this pesto will stay sweet and delicious in the refrigerator for up to one month. Otherwise, make the pesto just before serving to prevent any bitterness.

Makes about 2 cups

- 1 cup packed fresh oregano or marjoram leaves
- 4 small garlic cloves
- 1 cup walnut halves
- 1/2 cup freshly grated Parmesan or Romano cheese
- 6 tablespoons warm water
- 6 tablespoons whipping cream
- 1/2 cup virgin olive oil

With mortar and pestle: Combine oregano or marjoram and garlic in mortar and crush to fine paste. Gradually add walnut halves and work into paste. Add cheese and blend well. Slowly add water, cream and olive oil to mixture one at a time, stirring constantly until blended. Serve at room temperature.

With processor: Combine oregano or marjoram and garlic in work bowl and blend to fine paste, scraping down sides of bowl as necessary. Add walnut halves and blend to paste. Add cheese and mix well. Blend in water and cream. With machine running, pour olive oil through feed tube in slow steady stream and process until smooth. Serve at room temperature.

Pesto-Filled Won Ton Ravioli

8 to 10 servings

8 ounces ricotta cheese
1/4 cup pesto sauce (preferably homemade)
24 won ton wrappers

Pimiento Dressing
1/3 cup olive oil
2 tablespoons white wine vinegar
2 tablespoons chopped pimiento
1 garlic clove, minced
Salt and freshly ground pepper

1 large daikon (Japanese white radish),* peeled and grated
1/2 cup toasted pine nuts
Fresh basil leaves

Combine ricotta and pesto in medium bowl. Top each won ton wrapper with heaping teaspoon of ricotta mixture. Brush borders with water. Fold diagonally to form triangles, pressing edges firmly to seal.

Bring 1 1/2 inches of water to boil in bottom of wok or steamer. Lightly oil steamer rack and set over water, making sure rack does not touch water. Arrange some ravioli on rack; do not crowd. Cover and steam 5 minutes. Remove and set aside. Repeat with remaining ravioli. Cool completely.

For dressing: Combine olive oil, vinegar, pimiento and garlic in small bowl and mix well. Season with salt and pepper.

Spread daikon on serving platter. Pour half of dressing over. Arrange ravioli atop daikon. Drizzle with remaining dressing. Garnish with pine nuts and basil leaves and serve.

*Available at oriental markets and specialty produce stores.

Spaghetti with Asparagus

A specialty of Lanterna Blu, a picturesque sidewalk cafe in Imperia, Italy.

4 servings

1/4 cup (1/2 stick) butter
1 1/2 tablespoons olive oil
1/2 onion, thinly sliced
1 slice prosciutto, chopped
8 ounces asparagus, cut into slivers
1/2 cup water
1 chicken bouillon cube or 1 teaspoon chicken stock base
8 ounces thin spaghetti or vermicelli
1/2 cup half and half
1/4 cup freshly grated Parmesan cheese
Freshly ground pepper

Heat butter and oil in 1-quart saucepan over medium-high heat. Add onion and sauté until golden (do not brown). Add prosciutto and sauté briefly. Add asparagus, water and bouillon cube. Reduce heat and simmer about 15 minutes.

Add spaghetti to large pot of rapidly boiling salted water and cook until al dente, about 5 to 6 minutes. Drain well. Return spaghetti to pot. Add asparagus mixture and half and half and cook over medium-low heat until warmed through. Top with Parmesan and pepper before serving.

Broccoli Taglierini

6 servings

- 1 pound fresh broccoli (use florets only) or one 10-ounce package frozen broccoli spears
- ½ cup (1 stick) butter
- 1 garlic clove, halved
- 8 ounces taglierini or fettuccine, freshly cooked and drained
- 1 cup freshly grated Parmesan cheese

Cook florets in boiling salted water to cover until crisp-tender, or cook frozen broccoli according to package directions. Drain well. Cut broccoli spears into smaller pieces.

Melt butter with garlic in large skillet over medium heat; remove garlic. Add pasta and toss lightly until well coated. Add broccoli and toss again. Blend in cheese and serve.

Pasta with Artichoke Hearts

Serve as a salad or garnish with salami for a satisfying entrée.

4 servings

- 1 1-pound can artichoke hearts, drained, patted dry and cut lengthwise into ¼-inch slices
- ½ cup sliced black olives
- ¼ cup olive oil
- 3 tablespoons fresh lemon juice
- 2 garlic cloves, minced
- ⅛ teaspoon crumbled dried red chili
- Salt and freshly ground pepper
- 1 pound linguine, freshly cooked and drained
- Sliced Italian hard salami, cut into julienne (optional garnish)

Combine artichoke hearts, olives, oil, lemon juice, garlic, red pepper, salt and pepper in medium bowl. Let stand at room temperature for at least 1 hour.

Combine linguine and sauce in shallow large serving bowl and toss well. Garnish with salami and serve immediately.

Artichoke Linguine

4 servings

- ¼ cup (½ stick) butter
- ¼ cup olive oil
- 1 tablespoon all purpose flour
- 1 cup chicken stock
- 1 garlic clove, crushed
- 1 tablespoon minced fresh parsley
- 2 to 3 teaspoons fresh lemon juice
- Salt and freshly ground white pepper
- 1 14-ounce can artichoke hearts packed in water, drained and sliced
- 2 tablespoons freshly grated Parmesan cheese
- 2 teaspoons capers, rinsed and drained
- 1 tablespoon butter
- 2 tablespoons olive oil
- 1 tablespoon freshly grated Parmesan cheese
- ¼ teaspoon salt
- 1 pound linguine, freshly cooked and drained
- 2 ounces prosciutto or other ham, minced (garnish)

Melt butter with oil in small saucepan over medium heat. Add flour and stir until smooth, about 3 minutes. Blend in stock, stirring until thickened, about 1 minute. Reduce heat to low. Add garlic, parsley, lemon juice, salt and pepper and cook about 5 minutes, stirring constantly. Blend in artichokes, cheese and capers. Cover and simmer about 8 minutes.

Melt remaining butter in large skillet over medium heat. Stir in remaining oil, cheese and salt. Add linguine and toss lightly. Arrange pasta on platter and pour sauce over. Garnish with prosciutto.

Spicy Broccoli-Orzo Salad

4 servings

- **2½ cups steamed broccoli florets**
- **8 ounces orzo (rice-shaped pasta), freshly cooked and drained**
- **2 large tomatoes, chopped**
- **3 medium-size green onions, chopped**
- **3 tablespoons chopped fresh parsley**
- **1 tablespoon olive oil**
- **1 tablespoon red wine vinegar**
- **1 teaspoon salt**
- **1 teaspoon freshly ground pepper**
- **1 teaspoon garlic powder**

Combine all ingredients in large bowl and toss. Cover and refrigerate overnight. Serve slightly chilled or at room temperature.

Lemon Tagliolini with Fresh Basil Sauce

4 servings

- **¼ cup olive oil**
- **2 tablespoons fresh lemon juice**
- **1½ tablespoons minced fresh basil or 1 teaspoon dried, crumbled**
- **1 teaspoon minced lemon peel**
- **1 garlic clove, minced**
- **Salt and freshly ground pepper**
- **1 tablespoon olive or vegetable oil**
- **½ recipe Lemon Tagliolini (see page 5)**

Combine all ingredients except 1 tablespoon oil and pasta.

Bring large amount of salted water to rapid boil in large pot. Stir in 1 tablespoon oil. Add pasta and stir vigorously to prevent sticking. Cook until just firm but almost tender to the bite (al dente), about 2 minutes. Drain well. Toss with sauce. Serve pasta hot, warm or at room temperature.

Eggplant and Macaroni Casserole

6 servings

- **1 1-pound eggplant, peeled and cut into ½-inch slices**
- **Vegetable or olive oil (optional)**
- **2 tablespoons (¼ stick) butter**
- **1 medium onion, cut into ¼-inch dice**
- **1 28-ounce can tomatoes, seeded and coarsely chopped (reserve liquid)**
- **1 bay leaf**
- **¼ teaspoon dried thyme, crumbled**
- **Salt and freshly ground pepper**
- **8 ounces elbow macaroni, freshly cooked and drained**
- **8 ounces mozzarella cheese, coarsely grated**
- **2 tablespoons freshly grated Parmesan cheese**

Preheat oven to 375°F. Grease baking sheet. Brush eggplant lightly on both sides with oil, if desired. Arrange in single layer on prepared sheet. Bake until tender and lightly browned, turning once, about 15 minutes per side. Set aside. (Retain oven temperature at 375°F.)

Meanwhile, melt butter in medium skillet over medium heat. Add onion and cook until tender, about 7 minutes. Stir in tomatoes with liquid, bay leaf and thyme. Season with salt and pepper. Simmer until liquid is evaporated, stirring occasionally, about 30 minutes. Remove bay leaf and discard.

Grease 2- to 2½-quart baking dish. Combine tomato mixture, macaroni and mozzarella cheese in large bowl. Layer half of eggplant in prepared dish. Cover with half of tomato-macaroni mixture. Repeat layering, then sprinkle with Parmesan cheese. Bake until cheese is melted and mixture is heated through, about 30 minutes. Serve immediately.

Pasta with Eggplant and Tomato Topping

8 servings

1 unpeeled large eggplant, cut into wedges to fit processor feed tube
2 teaspoons salt

3 tablespoons safflower oil
2 tablespoons olive oil
3 medium onions (12 ounces total), quartered and shredded
2 medium garlic cloves, minced
2 large tomatoes (13 ounces total), cored and coarsely chopped
2 cups fresh parsley leaves, minced
2 tablespoons red wine vinegar
1¼ teaspoons sugar
1 teaspoon dried oregano, crumbled
Salt and freshly ground pepper

Basic Processor Pasta (see page 2), freshly cooked and drained
3 tablespoons olive oil
2 ounces Parmesan cheese, shredded (optional)

Using food processor fitted with French fry disc, position eggplant in feed tube and cut using medium pressure. Transfer to colander, sprinkle with salt and toss lightly. Weight down with plate and let stand for 30 minutes to drain. Pat dry with paper towels.

Heat oils in large skillet over medium heat. Add onion and garlic and sauté until softened, about 10 minutes. Add eggplant and cook until tender, shaking pan constantly to avoid sticking or burning. Add tomatoes, parsley, vinegar, sugar, oregano, salt and pepper and heat through, stirring gently with wooden spoon. Remove from heat.

Toss pasta with remaining olive oil. Add topping and toss again. Taste and adjust seasoning. Sprinkle with shredded Parmesan and serve.

Green Pasta with Leeks

6 to 8 servings

Pasta
1 cup fresh spinach leaves (1 ounce), well dried and minced
1 medium-size green onion (½ ounce), minced
2 tablespoons minced fresh parsley
3 eggs
2½ cups unbleached all purpose flour
1 teaspoon salt

Leeks
6 tablespoons (¾ stick) unsalted butter
3 medium leeks including tops (1 pound total), thinly sliced
1¼ cups whipping cream
1½ teaspoons salt
Freshly ground pepper
Freshly grated nutmeg

2 tablespoons salt
1 6-ounce can pitted extra-large black olives, drained and slivered

For pasta: Combine spinach, onion and parsley and mix well. Add eggs and mix thoroughly. Add 2 cups flour with salt and mix until dough forms ball. If necessary, add remaining flour by tablespoons and mix until dough is smooth and moist but not wet. Wrap in plastic and let rest for 30 minutes.

Place dough on well-floured board and cut into 8 pieces. Working with 1 piece at a time (leave remainder covered with plastic to prevent drying), by hand or machine roll and stretch dough into rectangle about 1/16 inch thick, adding flour only as necessary.

Using pasta machine: Set rollers for widest setting. Lightly flour 1 piece of dough. Run through rollers once, flour lightly, fold into thirds and run through rollers again, pulling dough gently to stretch as it comes out of machine. Repeat folding and rolling, lightly flouring only when necessary, until pasta is smooth as suede. *(This may take 6 or more rollings.)*

Reset rollers for next thinner setting. Lightly flour pasta, but do not fold, and run through machine again. Repeat on each thinner setting until as thin as desired. Brush off any excess flour. Repeat with remaining dough. Allow pasta to rest on towel until taut but not dry. Cut pasta on noodle or vermicelli setting. Separate strands and dry completely on cloth or cloth-covered pole.

By hand: On lightly floured board roll each piece of dough into as thin a rectangle as desired, adding flour only as necessary. Brush off excess flour with soft pastry brush, leaving only very thin layer of flour. Starting with short end, roll up dough like jelly roll. Using sharp knife, cut into 1/4-inch widths for noodles or 1/16-inch widths for vermicelli. Carefully unroll strands and dry completely on cloth or cloth-covered pole.

About 30 minutes before serving, prepare leeks: Melt 3 tablespoons butter in 2-quart saucepan over medium heat. Add leeks and cook, stirring occasionally, until softened but not browned, about 10 minutes. Blend in cream and cook uncovered over medium heat, stirring frequently, until thickened, about 10 minutes. Add salt, pepper and nutmeg. Remove from heat and keep hot.

Add pasta to 6 quarts rapidly boiling water with 2 tablespoons salt. When water returns to boil, cook just until pasta is al dente, about 1 to 2 minutes; *pasta cooks quickly so check often.* Drain. Transfer to heated serving platter, add leeks and remaining 3 tablespoons butter and toss lightly. Garnish with olives, mixing only slightly into pasta.

Entire dish can be prepared 1 day before serving. Cook pasta until barely al dente. Before reheating bring to room temperature, then reheat in large saucepan, stirring gently.

Pasta with Mediterranean Sauce

4 servings

1 6-ounce can pitted large black olives, drained and sliced
1/2 cup olive oil
1/2 cup freshly grated Parmesan cheese
1 teaspoon *each* minced fresh oregano, basil, thyme and sage
1 teaspoon freshly ground pepper
1 pound pasta, freshly cooked and drained
Tomato slices (garnish)

Combine olives, olive oil, cheese, oregano, basil, thyme, sage and pepper in medium bowl and mix well. Let stand at room temperature for 1 hour.

Place pasta in shallow large serving bowl and pour sauce over top. Surround with tomato slices and serve.

Orange Pappardelle with Fresh Spinach, Mushroom and Cream Sauce

4 servings

- 1/4 cup (1/2 stick) butter
- 1 large garlic clove, minced
- 2 tablespoons Marsala
- 8 ounces mushrooms, thinly sliced and tossed with 1 tablespoon fresh lemon juice
- 1 cup whipping cream
- Salt and freshly ground pepper

- 1 tablespoon olive or vegetable oil
- 1/2 recipe Orange Pappardelle (see page 6)
- 1 tablespoon butter
- 12 ounces fresh spinach, stemmed and thinly sliced
- 1/3 cup freshly grated Parmesan cheese
- Additional freshly grated Parmesan cheese

Melt butter in medium skillet over medium heat. Add garlic and Marsala and simmer until syrupy, about 3 minutes. Add mushrooms and cook until liquid is released, about 3 minutes. Add cream and bring just to boil. Season with salt and generous amount of pepper. Remove sauce from heat.

Bring large amount of salted water to rapid boil in large pot. Add oil. Add pasta and stir vigorously to prevent sticking. Cook until just firm but almost tender to the bite (at dente), about 3 minutes. Drain well. Return pasta to pot. Toss with 1 tablespoon butter. Warm sauce over high heat. Toss with pasta. Add fresh spinach and toss again. Sprinkle with 1/3 cup cheese and serve immediately. Pass additional Parmesan cheese separately.

Piccagge with Mushroom Sauce (Piccagge con Sugo di Funghi)

Piccagge, which means "napkins" in Genoese dialect, are similar in shape to narrow lasagne noodles.

4 to 6 servings

Piccagge

- 3 cups all purpose flour, preferably unbleached
- 4 eggs, room temperature

Mushroom Sauce

- 2 ounces porcini (dried Italian mushrooms)*

- 1/4 cup olive oil
- 1 medium onion, finely chopped
- 2 medium garlic cloves, finely chopped
- 4 large tomatoes, peeled, cored, seeded and finely diced
- 1 tablespoon tomato paste
- Salt and freshly ground pepper

- 1 tablespoon olive or vegetable oil

For piccagge: Arrange flour in mound on work surface and make well in center. Break eggs into well and blend with fork. Gradually draw small amount of flour from inner edge of well into eggs with fork, stirring constantly until all flour is incorporated. Gather dough into loose mass and set aside. Scrape any hard bits of flour from work surface and discard. Lightly flour work surface and hands. Knead dough until smooth and elastic, 10 to 12 minutes. Insert finger in center of dough; if dry, dough is ready for pasta machine; if sticky, sprinkle dough lightly with flour and continue kneading until dough is correct consistency.

Cut off 1 egg-size piece of dough. Store remaining dough in plastic wrap or dry towel to prevent drying; set aside. Flatten piece of dough with heel of hand, then fold in half. Turn pasta machine to widest setting and run dough through. Continue folding and kneading process with pasta machine until dough is smooth and velvety, about 2 more times (number will depend on how vigorously dough was kneaded by hand). Dust dough lightly with more flour as necessary.

Adjust pasta machine to next narrower setting. Run dough through machine *without folding,* dusting lightly with flour if sticky. Repeat, narrowing rollers after each run until machine is on second to narrowest setting; pasta should be less than 1/16 inch thick.

Knead and shape remaining dough into sheets, kneading each egg-size piece of dough slightly before running through machine. Set aside until sheets look firm and leathery and edges begin to curl up slightly but are not brittle. This will take 10 to 30 minutes depending on dryness of dough and temperature and humidity of kitchen. *Pasta must be cut at this point or dough will be too brittle.*

Cut 1 dough sheet into 2½ × 5-inch strips using fluted pastry wheel. Transfer piccagge to kitchen towel set on baking sheet. Repeat with remaining sheets of dough. *(Piccagge can be left overnight to dry in a cool dry place.)*

For sauce: Combine mushrooms in small bowl with just enough lukewarm water to cover. Let stand until softened, about 30 minutes. Drain mushrooms well and squeeze dry, reserving liquid. Strain liquid through several layers of cheesecloth; set aside. Discard hard stems; dice mushroom caps.

Heat ¼ cup oil in medium saucepan over medium-low heat. Add onion, cover and cook until pale yellow, 10 minutes. Add garlic, tomato and mushrooms and blend well. Dilute tomato paste in small amount of reserved mushroom liquid. Stir mixture (and remaining mushroom liquid) into saucepan. Bring to simmer and cook, stirring constantly, until reduced to saucelike consistency, about 25 minutes. Season with salt and pepper. Set aside.

Fill pasta cooker or stockpot ¾ full with salted water and bring to rapid boil over high heat. Stir in 1 tablespoon oil. Add piccagge and stir vigorously to prevent sticking. Cook until just firm but tender to bite (al dente), about 5 to 20 seconds for freshly made and up to 3 minutes for thoroughly dried pasta. Taste often to prevent overcooking. Drain. Place sauce over high heat and stir until hot. Add pasta to sauce and blend gently. Transfer to heated platter and serve.

*Four ounces fresh mushrooms, sliced, can be substituted for dried. Sauté in 1 tablespoon butter over medium-high heat until golden, about 5 minutes. Add to sauce during last 5 minutes of cooking.

Pasta with Mushroom and Zucchini Topping

6 to 8 servings

6 tablespoons (¾ stick) unsalted butter
3 medium garlic cloves, minced
1 pound mushrooms, sliced
2 tablespoons fresh lemon juice
4 small unpeeled zucchini (1 pound total), cut into ¼-inch-wide julienne
4 tablespoons minced fresh parsley
1 to 2 teaspoons dried basil, crumbled
1½ teaspoons salt
Freshly ground pepper
1 pound freshly cooked pasta (preferably homemade)

Melt 2 tablespoons butter in large skillet over medium heat. Add 1 garlic clove and cook 3 minutes. Add mushrooms and lemon juice and toss until well combined. Add zucchini, 2 tablespoons parsley and seasonings and blend well. Cover, increase heat to medium-high and cook until vegetables are steamed through, about 3 to 5 minutes, shaking pan frequently.

Place remaining butter and garlic in large serving bowl. Add hot pasta and remaining parsley and toss well. Top with vegetables and toss again. Taste and adjust seasoning.

Strichetti with Onion and Pea Sauce (Strichetti con Cipolla e Pisellini)

6 servings

Butterfly Pasta

3 cups all purpose flour, preferably unbleached
4 eggs, room temperature

Onion and Pea Sauce

1/4 cup (1/2 stick) butter
4 ounces pancetta or bacon, diced
2 large sweet yellow onions, diced
1/2 cup fresh peas (about 8 ounces unshelled)*
Salt and freshly ground pepper

1 tablespoon olive or vegetable oil

3/4 cup (or more) freshly grated Parmesan cheese

For pasta: Arrange flour in mound on work surface and make well in center. Break eggs into well and blend with fork. Gradually draw small amount of flour from inner edge of well into eggs with fork, stirring constantly until all flour is incorporated. Gather dough into loose mass and set aside. Scrape any hard bits of flour from work surface and discard. Lightly flour work surface and hands. Knead dough until smooth and elastic, 10 to 12 minutes. Insert finger in center of dough; if dry, dough is ready for pasta machine; if sticky, sprinkle dough lightly with flour and continue kneading until dough is correct consistency.

To knead and shape dough in pasta machine: Cut off 1 egg-size piece of dough. Store remaining dough in plastic wrap or dry towel to prevent drying; set aside. Flatten piece of dough with heel of hand, then fold in half. Turn pasta machine to widest setting and run dough through. Continue folding and kneading process with pasta machine until dough is smooth and velvety, about 2 more times (number will depend on how vigorously dough was kneaded by hand). Dust dough lightly with more flour as necessary.

Adjust pasta machine to next narrower setting. Run dough through machine *without folding,* dusting lightly with flour if sticky. Repeat, narrowing rollers after each run until machine is on second to narrowest setting; pasta should be less than 1/16 inch thick.

To form butterfly, immediately cut dough sheet into 1 1/2 × 2-inch rectangles. Pinch long sides of rectangle together in center. Transfer to kitchen towel set on baking sheet. Set aside at room temperature to dry until ready to cook. Repeat with remaining pieces of dough.

For sauce: Melt butter in large skillet over medium heat. Add pancetta and cook until meat just begins to color, about 5 minutes. Reduce heat to medium-low and stir in onion and peas. Cover and cook until onion and peas are tender, about 15 minutes, stirring occasionally. Taste sauce and season with salt and pepper. Set aside.

Fill pasta cooker or stockpot 3/4 full with salted water and bring to rapid boil over high heat. Stir in oil. Add pasta and stir vigorously to prevent sticking. Cook until just firm but tender to bite (al dente), about 5 to 20 seconds for freshly made and up to 3 minutes for thoroughly dried pasta. Taste often to prevent overcooking. Drain.

Add pasta to sauce. Sprinkle with 3/4 cup Parmesan. Place over low heat and mix gently until sauce is heated through and pasta is well coated. Transfer to heated platter and serve. Pass additional Parmesan separately, if desired.

*Thawed tiny frozen peas can be substituted for fresh. Stir into cooked onion and proceed with recipe as instructed.

Green Fettuccine with Prosciutto and Peas

2 servings

Sauce
- 1 tablespoon olive oil
- 1 tablespoon butter
- 1/2 cup chicken stock
- 1 small garlic clove, minced
- 1/4 cup freshly grated Parmesan cheese
- 1 10-ounce package frozen tiny peas
- Salt and freshly ground white pepper

- 4 ounces green fettuccine
- 1 tablespoon olive oil
- 1 tablespoon butter
- 1/4 cup freshly grated Parmesan cheese
- 1 ounce prosciutto or other thinly sliced ham, cut into short strips 1/4 inch wide
- Freshly grated Parmesan cheese

For sauce: Heat 1 tablespoon each oil and butter in medium saucepan over medium heat. Add stock and garlic and bring to simmer. Add 1/4 cup Parmesan and cook, stirring constantly, until cheese is melted and sauce is slightly thickened, about 5 to 10 minutes. Add peas and continue cooking until barely tender. Season with salt and white pepper. Keep warm.

Cook pasta in large amount of rapidly boiling water until at dente. Drain well. Return pasta to pot with remaining oil and butter and toss until butter is melted. Add 1/4 cup Parmesan and toss again. Season with salt and pepper. Turn into heated serving dish. Top with sauce and sprinkle with prosciutto. Serve with additional Parmesan.

Green Pea Farfalle with Peas, Green Onion and Mint

6 servings

- 1/4 cup (1/2 stick) butter
- 3 tablespoons pancetta, cut into 1/4-inch dice
- 1 10-ounce package frozen tiny peas, thawed, or 2 pounds young fresh peas, shelled
- 1/2 cup thinly sliced green onion
- 1/4 cup minced fresh mint leaves
- Salt and freshly ground pepper

- 1 tablespoon olive or vegetable oil
- 1/2 recipe Green Pea Farfalle (see page 5)

Melt butter in heavy medium skillet over low heat. Add pancetta and sauté 1 minute. Add frozen peas, onion, mint, salt and pepper. Cover and cook until peas are tender, about 3 minutes. *(For fresh peas, add peas, salt and pepper. Cover and cook until peas are tender, 15 to 30 minutes depending on size; add onion and mint during last 3 minutes.)* Set aside.

Bring large amount of salted water to rapid boil in large pot. Stir in oil. Add pasta, stirring vigorously to prevent sticking. Cook until just firm but almost tender to the bite (al dente), about 4 minutes. Drain well. Reheat peas. Toss with pasta. Adjust seasoning and serve immediately.

Peppered Olive Sauce with Walnuts

Thick and crunchy, almost like a tapénade, this inspired combination goes well not only with pasta but also with baked potatoes, firm-fleshed fish and various egg dishes.

Makes 3 pints

- **2/3 cup olive oil**
- **1 large green bell pepper, cut into 1/8-inch dice**
- **1 large red bell pepper, cut into 1/8-inch dice**
- **1 medium-size yellow bell pepper, cut into 1/8-inch dice**
- **3 garlic cloves, minced**
- **2 cups finely diced black olives**
- **1 cup toasted walnuts, finely chopped**
- **2 teaspoons salt**
- **Freshly ground pepper**
- **1/2 cup balsamic vinegar**
- **1/2 cup Niçoise olives**
- **2/3 cup minced Italian parsley**
- **Olive oil**

Heat 2/3 cup olive oil in heavy large skillet over medium-high heat. Add green, red and yellow bell peppers and stir-fry 5 minutes. Add garlic and continue stir-frying until peppers are softened, about 5 minutes. Stir in black olives, walnuts, salt and pepper and cook until flavors are blended, about 10 minutes. Increase heat to medium-high, pour in vinegar and cook until only a small amount of liquid remains, about 5 minutes. Add Niçoise olives and heat through. Mix in parsley. Cool to room temperature. Transfer to jars. Cover with thin layer of olive oil; seal tightly. *(Can be prepared 2 weeks ahead and refrigerated.)* Bring to room temperature before serving.

Macaroni with Sauce Spiga (Salsa Spiga per Maccheroni)

2 servings

- **1 red or yellow bell pepper**
- **3 large ripe tomatoes**
- **1 garlic clove**
- **1/4 cup olive oil**
- **1 large onion, sliced**
- **3 green tomatoes, sliced**
- **Pinch of dried red chili**
- **Pinch of dried rosemary**
- **1 tablespoon minced fresh parsley**
- **Freshly ground pepper**
- **8 ounces shell macaroni, farfalle or other small pasta, freshly cooked and drained**

Preheat broiler. Broil pepper, turning to char evenly. Cool until easy to handle, then peel off skin. (This is an optional step and may be omitted if you do not mind the pepper skin.) Core pepper and slice into 1/2-inch strips.

Place ripe tomatoes in bowl and pour boiling water over. Let stand 1 minute, then peel and slice thickly.

Place garlic in 9-inch skillet and add oil. Set skillet over medium-high heat; as soon as garlic starts to sizzle, add onion and cook, stirring constantly, 10 minutes. Add pepper strips and cook until soft. Add ripe tomatoes and cook 5 minutes. Stir in green tomatoes, chili and rosemary and cook 5 minutes longer. Add parsley and a pinch of pepper. Remove skillet from heat and discard garlic. Pour sauce over cooked pasta and serve immediately.

Red on Red Sauce

A delightful chunky sauce—for pasta, rice, poultry or fish—that can also be served as a side dish. Prepare this in quantity during the summer and freeze for winter.

4 servings

- 3 tablespoons olive oil
- 2 large red bell peppers or 6 sweet red Italian peppers, seeded and cut into thin strips
- 1 large onion, cut into thin strips
- 1/2 cup tightly packed chopped fresh basil leaves or 3 tablespoons dried, crumbled
- 1 large garlic clove, minced
- 4 large ripe tomatoes, cored, seeded and chopped
- 1 3x1/4-inch strip orange peel
- Salt and freshly ground pepper

Heat olive oil in large skillet over medium heat. Add pepper and onion strips and cook until onion is soft and translucent. Stir in basil and garlic and cook 1 minute. Add tomatoes and orange peel. Increase heat to high and cook, stirring constantly, until mixture thickens, about 3 minutes. Remove from heat and season with salt and pepper to taste. Transfer to container and refrigerate. *(Can be refrigerated for several days or frozen up to 3 months.)*

Linguine with Paprika Sauce (Linguine con Salsa Paprica)

A colorful, easy-to-make first course.

4 servings

- 1/2 cup olive oil
- 4 garlic cloves, crushed
- 1/4 cup Hungarian sweet paprika
- 1/2 cup dry white wine
- 4 medium tomatoes, peeled and seeded, or 3/4 cup well-drained canned Italian plum tomatoes
- 1/2 teaspoon salt
- 1 pound linguine
- 2 tablespoons olive oil
- 1 1/2 cups (4 ounces) freshly grated pecorino Romano cheese
- Additional freshly grated pecorino Romano cheese

Heat 1/2 cup oil in heavy 10-inch skillet over low heat. Add garlic and cook until golden brown, about 10 minutes. Discard garlic using slotted spoon. Add paprika to skillet and stir 5 minutes. Add wine. Increase heat and boil until reduced by half. Finely chop tomatoes in processor or blender. Add to skillet. Stir in salt. Simmer until sauce thickens, about 10 minutes.

Meanwhile, cook linguine in large pot of rapidly boiling salted water until just tender but firm to bite. Drain. Place 2 tablespoons oil on heated platter and add pasta. Spoon sauce over top. Sprinkle with 1 1/2 cups cheese and toss to blend. Serve immediately. Pass additional cheese separately.

Fettuccine con Radicchio

An elegant pasta dish from Valentino, one of Los Angeles's premier Italian restaurants.

4 to 6 servings

- 2 pounds spinach fettuccine
- 1/4 cup (1/2 stick) butter
- 4 ounces slab bacon, cut into 1/3-inch dice
- 1/2 cup dry white wine
- Salt and freshly ground pepper
- 1 large head radicchio,* cut lengthwise into eighths
- 3/4 cup veal stock
- 3/4 cup Valentino's Basic Tomato Sauce**
- Freshly grated Parmesan cheese

Bring large amount of salted water to rapid boil in large saucepan. Stir in fettuccine and cook until firm but tender to the bite (al dente). Drain well.

Melt butter in deep large skillet over medium heat. Add bacon and stir until cooked through but not crisp, 2 to 3 minutes. Drain almost all fat from skillet.

Return skillet to medium heat. Add wine with salt and pepper to taste, stirring up any browned bits. Stir in radicchio and cook until just soft. Add stock and cook 1 minute. Blend in tomato sauce. Add pasta and toss gently. Sprinkle generously with Parmesan cheese. Serve immediately.

*A bitter red winter chicory native to Treviso and available in specialty produce markets. Belgian endive can be substituted.

**Valentino's Basic Tomato Sauce

Makes 2½ cups

2 tablespoons olive oil
¾ cup chopped onion
1 teaspoon minced garlic
4 pounds tomatoes (preferably Italian plum tomatoes), peeled, seeded and chopped
2 tablespoons dried basil, crumbled
Salt and freshly ground pepper

Heat oil in large skillet over medium-high heat. Add onion and garlic. Reduce heat to low, cover and cook until translucent, about 10 minutes. Blend in tomatoes. Increase heat to medium-low and cook until mixture begins to thicken, stirring frequently. Add basil, reduce heat to low and simmer until thick. Season sauce with salt and pepper.

Raisin and Pine Nut Vinaigrette

Drizzle this intriguing dressing over pasta, grilled fish or chicken, cold shellfish or cooked vegetables.

Makes 1¼ cups

⅓ cup raisins, rinsed in warm water
¼ cup dry Sherry

3 tablespoons Sherry vinegar
1 teaspoon sugar
1 small garlic clove, minced
Salt and freshly ground pepper
⅔ cup olive oil
⅓ cup toasted pine nuts
2½ tablespoons minced fresh herbs (parsley, thyme, oregano, marjoram)
2 tablespoons minced green onion

Soak raisins in Sherry 30 minutes.

Drain raisins, reserving liquid. Blend vinegar, sugar, garlic, salt and pepper in small bowl. Whisk in olive oil 1 drop at a time. Whisk in 1 to 1½ tablespoons reserved liquid. Mix in pine nuts, herbs, green onion and raisins. Let stand at room temperature 2 hours. Whisk before serving.

Ukrainian Spinach and Noodles

2 servings

1 cup freshly cooked egg noodles
3 tablespoons butter
¼ cup chopped onion
1 10-ounce bunch fresh spinach, rinced, dried, stemmed and torn into bite-size pieces, or one 10-ounce package frozen spinach, thawed, squeezed dry and chopped
¼ cup grated Swiss or Gruyère cheese (1 ounce)
Salt and freshly ground pepper

Toss warm cooked noodles with 1 tablespoon butter. Melt remaining butter in large skillet over medium-low heat. Add onion and cook until tender, about 5 minutes. Add spinach, increase heat to high and cook until spinach is limp and moisture has evaporated, tossing occasionally. Add noodles to skillet and toss gently until heated through. Transfer to heated bowl. Add cheese and season with salt and pepper. Toss gently and serve.

Egg Pasta, Spinach and Herbs

8 servings

Pasta

1 1/2 cups unbleached all purpose flour
2 eggs
2 egg yolks
1 teaspoon salt
2 teaspoons vegetable or olive oil

Spinach Mixture

1 1/2 pounds fresh spinach, including stems (2 cups cooked)

5 large shallots (2 ounces)

6 tablespoons (3/4 stick) unsalted butter

1/4 cup fresh parsley leaves
1 teaspoon salt
1/2 teaspoon dried oregano, crumbled
1/2 teaspoon dried basil, crumbled
1/2 teaspoon freshly grated nutmeg
Freshly ground black pepper

2 tablespoons salt

For pasta: Place all ingredients except oil in food processor fitted with steel knife. Combine with on/off turns, then process until dough masses together. Add oil and process until mixture forms a ball. Process an additional 20 to 30 seconds to knead. If dough is too sticky, add more flour 1 tablespoon at a time. Wrap dough in plastic and let rest 30 minutes at room temperature.

Place dough on well-floured board and cut into 8 pieces. (To prevent drying, cover remaining pieces with plastic as you work.) By hand or machine, roll and stretch out each piece into a rectangular shape 1/8 inch thick, adding more flour only as necessary.

Using pasta machine: Set rollers for widest setting. Lightly flour piece of dough to be rolled first. Run through rollers once, flour lightly, fold into thirds and run through again. Repeat folding and rolling, lightly flouring only when necessary, until pasta is smooth as suede. *(This may take 6 or more rollings.)*

Reset rollers for next thinner setting. Lightly flour pasta but do not fold. Run through machine, repeating on each thinner setting until as thin as desired. Brush off any excess flour. Repeat with remaining 7 pieces of dough.

Allow pasta to rest on towel until taut but not dry. Cut on noodle or vermicelli setting and allow to dry on a cloth or on a cloth-covered rack. In either case, separate the strands.

By hand: On floured board, roll each piece into as thin a rectangle as possible. Starting with short end, roll up dough like jelly roll. Cut dough into noodles 1/8 to 1/4 inch wide. Allow to dry completely on towel.

For spinach mixture: Wash spinach thoroughly. Cook over medium-high heat using only the water clinging to leaves, stirring twice to cook evenly. As soon as it wilts, transfer to colander and hold under cold running water until spinach is cold to the touch. Drain well. Squeeze out excess moisture.

Mince shallots by dropping into processor feed tube with machine running.

Melt butter in 2-quart saucepan until sizzling. Add shallot and sauté 1 minute. Remove pan from heat.

Combine spinach with remaining ingredients and mix in processor with 5 on/off turns, then puree, stopping once to scrape down sides of work bowl.

Combine 4 quarts water with salt in large stockpot and bring to rapid boil. Add pasta. After it returns to boil, cook just until pasta is al dente (firm to the bite), about 30 seconds. Drain. Return saucepan with shallot to medium-high heat. When hot, add spinach mixture and heat through but *do not overcook.* Toss with pasta and taste for seasoning. Serve immediately.

Quick Herbed Tomato Sauce

Makes about 2 cups

- 1 tablespoon butter
- $1/2$ cup chopped onion
- 1 garlic clove, unpeeled
- 1 1-pound can Italian plum tomatoes (well drained), chopped
- Bouquet garni (2 thyme sprigs, 2 parsley sprigs and 1 bay leaf)
- 1 teaspoon sugar
- Salt and freshly ground pepper
- 1 tablespoon butter, cut into small pieces

Melt 1 tablespoon butter in medium skillet over medium heat. Add onion and garlic and cook, stirring occasionally, until golden. Discard garlic. Add tomatoes, bouquet garni and sugar. Cover and cook 30 minutes. Discard bouquet garni. Season to taste with salt and pepper. Pass mixture through food mill. If sauce is too thin, return to skillet and boil until reduced to desired thickness. *(Can be prepared ahead to this point, cooled, covered and refrigerated. Reheat before proceeding.)* Add remaining butter 1 piece at a time, whisking constantly until melted. Serve sauce immediately.

Basic Tomato Sauce

In this simple procedure, peeled, seeded and chopped tomatoes (what the French call tomates concassées*) are cooked slowly over very low heat to evaporate the liquid and concentrate flavor. A bit of butter whisked in at the end lends a creamy texture. The sauce can be seasoned a number of ways to suit a particular dish. For instance, mint and dill would lend a Middle Eastern tang; marjoram, oregano and basil give an Italian twist. Use as a garnish or as a sauce base for pasta, vegetables, fish, chicken or veal.*

Makes about $1\frac{1}{3}$ cups

- $1/4$ cup ($1/2$ stick) butter
- 3 tablespoons minced shallot (optional)
- 2 pounds tomatoes, peeled, seeded and juiced over strainer, then coarsely chopped
- 1 small garlic clove, minced (optional)
- Salt and freshly ground pepper
- Sugar (optional)
- $1/4$ cup minced fresh chervil or parsley
- $1\frac{1}{2}$ tablespoons minced fresh herbs or $1\frac{1}{2}$ teaspoons dried herbs, crumbled (optional)
- 2 to 3 tablespoons butter

Melt $1/4$ cup butter in heavy large saucepan over medium-low heat. Add shallot and stir until translucent, about 3 minutes. Mix in chopped tomatoes (and juice) and garlic. Cover and cook, stirring occasionally, until liquid evaporates and tomatoes are soft enough to mash with spoon (reducing heat to low and stirring frequently toward end of cooking time to prevent burning), about 40 minutes.* Season with salt and pepper. Taste and add sugar if necessary. Press sauce through sieve if smoother texture is desired. Stir in chervil and herbs. Just before serving, rewarm sauce over low heat and whisk in remaining butter 1 tablespoon at a time, blending well.

*Cooking time will vary depending on juiciness of tomatoes. You should have $1\frac{1}{3}$ cups of sauce at end of cooking period.

Uncooked Fresh Tomato Sauce

This easy sauce is a rosy accompaniment to pasta, cold meats, fish, chicken, vegetables and terrines. It can be stored in the refrigerator for up to three days. For best results, be sure tomato pulp is thoroughly squeezed before pureeing.

Makes about 1 cup

1 pound tomatoes, peeled, seeded, juiced and chopped
1½ teaspoons salt
¾ cup olive oil
2 tablespoons strained fresh lemon juice
1 tablespoon white wine vinegar
2 egg yolks, room temperature
Salt and freshly ground pepper
2 tablespoons minced fresh chives
2 tablespoons minced fresh chervil or parsley
1 tablespoon minced fresh herbs or 1 teaspoon dried, crumbled (optional)

Arrange tomatoes in colander and sprinkle with salt. Let drain 1 hour. Pat tomatoes with paper towels, then squeeze dry. Transfer to processor or blender. Add oil, lemon juice, vinegar and egg yolks and puree until smooth, stopping machine once to scrape down sides of container. Press sauce through sieve if desired. Season with salt and pepper. Just before serving, stir in minced chives, chervil and herbs.

Classic Tomato Sauce

This rich mixture simmers slowly in the oven for several hours to allow flavors to mellow. It is excellent with pasta, chicken or veal. If you wish, sauce can be lightly bound with flour to add body.

Makes about 1¾ cups

2 tablespoons (¼ stick) butter
1 tablespoon olive oil
1 small onion or leek (white part only), coarsely chopped
1 medium carrot, diced
1 celery stalk (with leaves), sliced
2 tablespoons minced ham, bacon, prosciutto or salt pork
1 small garlic clove, minced
1 tablespoon all purpose flour (optional)
2 pounds tomatoes, halved and pureed (do not sieve)*
1 cup chicken stock
½ cup mushroom trimmings (optional)
1 medium shallot, minced
1 bay leaf
6 parsley sprigs (with stems)
4 sprigs fresh thyme or 1 teaspoon dried, crumbled
3 leek greens (optional)
2 tablespoons Madeira, Cognac or Marsala (optional)
1 tablespoon minced fresh herbs (basil, thyme, oregano) or 1 teaspoon dried, crumbled (optional)
Sugar (optional)
Salt and freshly ground pepper

Preheat oven to 300°F. Heat butter and oil in heavy large ovenproof saucepan over medium-high heat. Reduce heat to low and add onion, carrot, celery, ham and garlic. Cover and cook, stirring occasionally, until onion is translucent, about 10 minutes. Add flour and stir 3 minutes. Blend in tomatoes, chicken stock, mushroom trimmings, shallot, bay leaf, parsley, thyme, leek greens, Madeira and herbs. Increase heat to medium and bring to boil. Cover, transfer to oven and bake until reduced and thickened, stirring occasionally, about 3 hours. Taste and add sugar if necessary. Strain sauce, pressing vegetables with back of wooden spoon to extract as much liquid as possible. Taste and season with salt and freshly ground pepper.

*For a lighter-textured sauce, peel and seed the tomatoes before pureeing.

Coriander-Cumin Tomato Sauce

Served hot or cold, this chunky green sauce makes a zesty topping for any cooked pasta.

Makes about 2 cups

½ cup packed fresh cilantro (coriander) leaves (about 1 large bunch)
⅓ cup packed fresh parsley leaves
1 to 2 green chilies, about 2¼ inches long (or more to taste), seeded
2 green onions, trimmed and quartered (or more to taste)

1 large garlic clove
4 tablespoons olive oil

1 to 1¼ teaspoons ground cumin
2 cups peeled chopped tomatoes
1 teaspoon tomato paste
Salt

Combine coriander, parsley, chilies, onion and garlic in processor and chop using on/off turns. Add 2 tablespoons olive oil and blend well. Transfer mixture to medium bowl and set aside.

Heat remaining 2 tablespoons oil with cumin in medium skillet over high heat until very hot. Add tomatoes and cook 30 seconds, shaking pan constantly. Stir in tomato paste. Remove from heat and cool. Add to coriander mixture, tossing gently to blend. Season with salt. Refrigerate before serving.

Herbed Tomato Sauce

Easy and quick, this light tomato sauce dresses up any kind of pasta.

Makes 1½ cups

1 tablespoon unsalted butter
1 tablespoon olive oil
1 small onion, chopped
5 large ripe tomatoes, peeled, seeded and coarsely chopped
2 teaspoons fresh lemon juice
1½ teaspoons sugar
6 fresh basil leaves
4 parsley sprigs
2 3-inch sprigs fresh thyme
1 medium garlic clove, chopped

Salt and freshly ground pepper
1½ teaspoons minced fresh basil
1 teaspoon minced fresh parsley

Melt butter with oil in heavy large saucepan over medium-low heat. Add onion, cover and cook until translucent, stirring occasionally, about 10 minutes. Add tomatoes, lemon juice, sugar, basil leaves, parsley and thyme sprigs and garlic and simmer until tomatoes are reduced to thick pulp, stirring occasionally, about 20 to 30 minutes.

Press sauce through fine sieve into nonaluminum bowl. Discard herbs. (If sauce is too thin, simmer gently in small saucepan to thicken, 10 to 20 minutes.) Season with salt and pepper. *(Can be prepared 2 days ahead and refrigerated. Rewarm over low heat.)* Mix in basil and parsley and serve.

Tomato Butter Sauce

The acid in the tomatoes helps bind the butter, making this the most foolproof of all butter sauces. Serve with pasta, fish, eggs, chicken or veal.

Makes about 1⅓ cups

1 tablespoon butter
1 cup chopped onion
2 garlic cloves, minced (1 scant tablespoon)
1½ pounds tomatoes, peeled, seeded, juiced and chopped (reserve juice)
1 bouquet garni (1 thyme sprig, 1 small bay leaf, 5 parsley stems)

1 cup (2 sticks) well-chilled unsalted butter, cut into ½-inch pieces

2 teaspoons tomato paste
Salt and freshly ground pepper

Melt 1 tablespoon butter in medium saucepan over low heat. Stir in onion, cover and cook until translucent, about 10 minutes. Add garlic and stir 30 seconds. Blend in tomato and bouquet garni. Increase heat to medium and cook until mixture is thick and reduced to about 1⅓ cups, about 25 minutes. *(Sauce can be prepared several hours ahead to this point. Transfer to small saucepan, discard bouquet garni and return to simmer before continuing with recipe.)*

Remove saucepan from heat. Add 2 pieces of chilled butter to reduction and whisk quickly until just incorporated. Place over low heat and whisk in remaining butter 1 piece at a time without stopping, adding each only after previous piece is just nearly incorporated; sauce should be thick and emulsified. (If at any time sauce becomes too hot and streaks or drops of melted butter appear, immediately remove sauce from heat and whisk in 2 pieces of butter. Continue whisking in butter 1 piece at a time, off heat, until sauce is thick and completely emulsified. Return sauce to low heat and continue whisking in butter 1 piece at a time.) Remove sauce from heat.

Strain 2 tablespoons reserved tomato juice into sauce. Strain sauce into another small saucepan, pressing on tomato with back of spoon to extract all liquid. Place over very low heat briefly just to rewarm, whisking constantly. Remove from heat. Whisk in tomato paste. Add salt and pepper; adjust seasoning. Serve immediately. *(Sauce can be held for a short period. Keep warm in vacuum bottle or on rack set above warm water, whisking sauce frequently to prevent any separation.)*

Pasta con Aglio

4 servings

4 tomatoes, peeled, seeded and coarsely chopped
½ cup olive oil
¼ cup fresh mint leaves, coarsely chopped
3 garlic cloves, minced
Salt and freshly ground pepper

1 pound pasta, freshly cooked and drained

Combine tomatoes, olive oil, mint, garlic, salt and pepper in small bowl and blend well. Let stand at room temperature for at least 2 hours.

Combine pasta and sauce in shallow large bowl, toss well and serve.

Spicy Clove Sauce

Finely crushed cloves give this dish an unusual and exciting flavor.

4 servings

6 to 8 medium tomatoes, peeled, seeded and cut into thin wedges
¾ cup olive oil
5 green onions, finely chopped
1 cup pitted black olives, coarsely chopped
1 tablespoon minced fresh oregano or 1½ teaspoons dried, crumbled
3 whole cloves, finely crushed

1 pound pasta, freshly cooked and drained
Freshly grated Romano cheese

Combine tomatoes, olive oil, onion, olives, oregano and cloves in large bowl and mix well. Let stand at room temperature for at least 2 hours.

Combine pasta and sauce in shallow large serving bowl and toss well. Sprinkle with grated Romano cheese and serve.

Capellini with Fresh Tomato and Basil Sauce

6 servings

- 2 pounds fresh plum tomatoes, peeled, seeded and coarsely chopped
- 1 cup coarsely chopped fresh basil leaves
- 1 3¼-ounce jar capers, rinsed and drained
- 3 tablespoons Sherry vinegar
- Salt and freshly ground pepper
- 1 pound capellini or angel hair pasta
- ¾ to 1 cup olive oil, preferably extra virgin

Combine tomatoes and basil. Marinate at room temperature 1 to 2 hours or overnight in refrigerator.

Blend capers, vinegar, salt and pepper into tomato mixture. Bring large amount of salted water to rapid boil. Add pasta and cook until al dente; drain well. Transfer to platter. Add enough oil to coat. Mix in tomato sauce. Let stand 5 minutes before serving.

Herb Pasta with Double Tomato Sauce

2 servings

- 1 egg
- 2 tablespoons chopped fresh parsley
- 1 tablespoon chopped fresh oregano or 1 teaspoon dried, crumbled
- 1 tablespoon chopped fresh thyme or 1 teaspoon dried, crumbled
- 1 cup all purpose flour
- 1 tablespoon olive oil
- ¾ teaspoon salt
- 2 teaspoons (about) water
- 3 tablespoons freshly grated Parmesan cheese
- 2 tablespoons (¼ stick) butter, melted
- Double Tomato Sauce*

Combine egg and herbs in processor and blend using on/off turns until herbs are minced and completely combined with egg. Add flour, oil and salt and blend well. Add water 1 teaspoon at a time and process until dough forms ball, using only enough water for dough to hold together.

Remove dough from work bowl and flour lightly. Run through pasta machine with rollers at widest setting. Fold dough in half, flour again and repeat rolling. Run through rollers at progressively narrower settings until pasta is desired thickness. Let dry on kitchen towels until firm but not brittle. Cut into noodles about ¼ inch wide. *(Herb pasta can be prepared ahead to this point and dried or frozen.)*

Bring large pot of salted water to rapid boil over high heat. Add pasta and cover pot just until water returns to boil. Uncover and boil until pasta is al dente, about 1 to 2 minutes. Drain in colander. Transfer to bowl. Add cheese and melted butter and toss gently. Divide between heated plates. Spoon on sauce and serve.

*Double Tomato Sauce

Makes ½ to ¾ cup

- 2 tablespoons olive oil
- 1 tablespoon butter
- ½ medium onion (about 2½ ounces), finely chopped
- 1 large tomato, peeled, seeded and chopped
- 1 tablespoon tomato paste
- 1 ounce sun-dried tomatoes (optional), patted dry and minced

Heat oil and butter in heavy medium skillet over low heat. Add onion and cook until translucent and very tender, about 15 minutes. Add chopped tomato and tomato paste. Increase heat to medium and cook until all liquid is absorbed and tomato is soft, about 20 minutes. Stir in minced dried tomatoes and serve.

Tomato Tagliolini with Tomatoes, Mozzarella and Basil

4 servings

3 large firm tomatoes, peeled, seeded and cut into 1/2-inch pieces
4 ounces mozzarella cheese (preferably fresh), cut into 1/4-inch dice
1/4 cup olive oil
2 tablespoons fresh lemon juice
1 tablespoon red wine vinegar
12 fresh basil leaves, coarsely chopped, or 1 teaspoon dried, crumbled
2 green onions, thinly sliced
1 medium garlic clove, minced
1/2 teaspoon fresh oregano or 1/4 teaspoon dried, crumbled
Salt and freshly ground pepper

1 tablespoon olive or vegetable oil
1/2 recipe Tomato Tagliolini (see page 8)
Chopped fresh basil leaves (garnish)

Combine all ingredients except 1 tablespoon oil, pasta and garnish in large serving bowl and toss gently.

Bring large amount of salted water to rapid boil in large pot. Add 1 tablespoon oil. Add pasta and stir vigorously to prevent sticking. Cook until just firm but almost tender to the bite (al dente), about 2 minutes. Drain well. Toss pasta with sauce. Season with salt and pepper. Serve hot or at room temperature. Top with basil.

Tomato and Mozzarella Sauce

4 servings

6 to 8 ripe tomatoes, peeled, seeded and coarsely chopped (reserve juice)
8 ounces mozzarella cheese, coarsely shredded
1/4 cup minced fresh basil leaves
5 tablespoons olive oil
2 garlic cloves, minced
1 tablespoon minced fresh parsley
Salt and freshly ground pepper

1 pound pasta, freshly cooked and drained

Combine tomatoes, reserved juice, cheese, basil, oil, garlic, parsley, salt and pepper in medium bowl and blend well. Let stand at room temperature 1 hour.

Combine pasta and sauce in shallow large serving bowl and toss until cheese is melted. Serve immediately.

Fresh Tomato and Green Olive Sauce

For best flavor, prepare the sauce at least two hours before serving.

4 servings

- **8 to 10 ripe tomatoes, peeled, seeded and cut into large chunks**
- **3/4 cup pitted large green olives, sliced**
- **3 garlic cloves, minced**
- **3 fresh oregano sprigs, minced, or 1 teaspoon dried, crumbled**
- **3 tablespoons minced fresh parsley**
- **Salt and freshly ground pepper**
- **1/2 cup olive oil**

- **1 pound pasta, freshly cooked and drained**

Combine tomatoes, olives, garlic, oregano, parsley, salt and pepper in large bowl. Add olive oil, mixing well. Cover and let stand at room temperature for at least 2 hours.

Combine pasta and sauce in shallow large serving bowl, toss well and serve.

Francis Coppola's Fusilli alla Pappone

A wonderful pasta dish that features fusilli (spiral macaroni) in a creamy zucchini and basil sauce with Parmesan cheese.

4 servings

- **Vegetable oil**
- **1 pound zucchini, cut into 3 × 1/8-inch strips**

- **1 pound fusilli**

- **3 tablespoons butter**
- **3 tablespoons olive oil**
- **1 teaspoon all purpose flour dissolved in 1/3 cup milk**
- **2/3 cup coarsely chopped fresh basil leaves**
- **1/4 teaspoon salt**
- **1 egg yolk, lightly beaten**
- **1/2 cup freshly grated Parmesan cheese**
- **1/4 cup freshly grated pecorino Romano cheese**

Heat 1/2 inch oil in medium skillet over medium-high heat. Add zucchini in small batches and sauté until lightly browned. Drain on paper towels.

Bring 4 quarts salted water to rapid boil. Add fusilli and cook al dente.

Heat 1 1/2 tablespoons butter with olive oil in large skillet over medium-high heat. When butter foams, reduce heat to medium-low and slowly stir in dissolved flour. Continue cooking, stirring constantly, 30 seconds. Add zucchini, stirring several times. Add basil and salt and cook briefly, stirring until heated through. Remove from heat and stir in remaining butter. Quickly beat in yolk and stir in cheese. Taste and adjust seasoning.

Drain pasta. Transfer to heated large serving bowl. Add sauce and toss thoroughly. Serve immediately.

Capellini Primavera La Camelia

8 to 10 first-course servings

- **1 tablespoon olive oil**
- **1/2 medium onion, coarsely chopped**
- **3 large tomatoes (1 1/2 pounds), peeled, seeded and chopped**
- **1 cup chicken stock**
- **1/2 cup whipping cream**

- **1 pound broccoli (florets only), coarsely chopped**
- **1 large carrot (4 ounces), cut into julienne**
- **1 pound capellini**
- **2 medium zucchini (about 12 ounces), peeled and cut into julienne**

- **1 1/2 cups freshly grated Parmesan cheese (3 ounces)**
- **1/4 cup (1/2 stick) unsalted butter**
- **Salt and freshly ground pepper**

Bring large pot of salted water to boil over high heat. Meanwhile, heat olive oil in large skillet over medium heat. Add onion and cook until lightly colored, about 5 minutes. Add tomatoes and cook 1 to 2 minutes, stirring. Mix in stock and cream. Remove sauce from heat and keep warm.

Add broccoli florets to boiling water. When water returns to boil, stir in carrot julienne and capellini. When water again returns to boil, cook 3 minutes, add zucchini julienne and continue cooking until pasta is al dente, about 2 to 3 more minutes. Drain well.

Transfer pasta mixture to large bowl. Add Parmesan and butter and toss to blend. Pour sauce over and toss gently. Season with salt and pepper. Serve immediately.

Pasta with Green Onion, Herbed Tomato and Kalamata Olive Topping

6 to 8 servings

18 small Italian plum tomatoes or 5 medium tomatoes, sliced
1/2 cup Kalamata olives, drained, pitted and sliced
2 teaspoons minced fresh basil or 1 teaspoon dried, crumbled
1 teaspoon sugar
1/2 teaspoon salt
Freshly ground pepper

1 garlic clove
1/2 cup fresh parsley leaves

3 to 4 ounces green onions, cut into thirds
3 tablespoons vegetable oil
3/4 teaspoon salt
Basic Processor Pasta (see page 2), cooked, drained and cooled to room temperature

Combine first 6 ingredients with pepper to taste in heavy-duty plastic bag and shake gently to mix. Refrigerate.

Mince garlic by dropping through processor feed tube with machine running. Add parsley and mince with on/off turns. Leave in work bowl.

Insert medium slicing blade into processor. Wedge onions vertically in feed tube and slice using light pressure. Transfer mixture to 1-quart bowl. Add oil, salt and pepper to taste and blend well. Add cooked pasta and toss thoroughly. Taste and adjust seasoning. Transfer to serving dish. Arrange tomato mixture around border. Serve at room temperature or chilled.

Vegetable Fettuccine Carbonara

6 servings

4 eggs
1/4 cup whipping cream
8 slices bacon, chopped
1/2 cup sliced mushrooms
1/2 cup sliced carrot
1/2 cup sliced cauliflower
1/2 cup frozen peas, thawed
1/2 cup sliced zucchini
1/2 red bell pepper, seeded and cut into 1-inch strips
1/4 cup sliced green onion
1 garlic clove, chopped

1 pound fettuccine
1/4 cup (1/2 stick) butter, cut into pieces
1 cup freshly grated Parmesan cheese
Salt and freshly ground pepper

Beat eggs with cream in small bowl and set aside. Cook bacon in heavy large skillet until crisp. Remove with slotted spoon and set aside. Add mushrooms, carrot, cauliflower, peas, zucchini, red bell pepper, onion and garlic to skillet and sauté until crisp-tender, about 5 to 7 minutes.

Meanwhile, cook fettuccine in large amount of boiling salted water until al dente. Drain well. Transfer to large serving bowl. Add butter and toss through. Add egg mixture and toss lightly. Add vegetables, bacon and cheese and toss again. Season with salt and pepper. Serve hot.

Pasta Garden

8 main-course servings

2 cups fresh parsley leaves
2 large garlic cloves
1 large onion (8 ounces), quartered

6 tablespoons (3/4 stick) unsalted butter

1 large red bell pepper (8 ounces), cored, seeded and cut into 2-inch rectangles
1 large green bell pepper (8 ounces), cored, seeded and cut into 2-inch rectangles

2 large zucchini (1 pound total), trimmed and cut into processor feed tube lengths
1 bunch broccoli (1 3/4 pounds), florets set aside, stems peeled

3 medium tomatoes (1 pound total), cored, halved and seeded
1 tablespoon Sherry vinegar
1 1/4 teaspoons salt
1/4 teaspoon dried oregano
1/4 teaspoon freshly grated nutmeg

6 quarts water
2 tablespoons salt
Tomato Basil Pasta (see page 7)

8 ounces Parmesan cheese, room temperature, shredded (2 cups)
2 ounces Romano cheese, room temperature, shredded (1/2 cup)
Freshly ground white pepper

In food processor fitted with steel knife, mince parsley using on/off turns. Remove and set aside. With machine running, drop garlic through feed tube and mince. Add onion to work bowl and chop finely.

Melt 3 tablespoons butter in 12-inch skillet or sauté pan over medium-low heat. Add garlic and onion and cook, stirring occasionally, until soft but not brown, about 8 to 10 minutes.

Insert thick or medium slicer into processor. Stand red and green pepper rectangles vertically in feed tube, packing tightly. Slice into matchsticks using light pressure.

Insert French fry disc. Stand zucchini vertically in feed tube and slice using medium pressure. Remove and set aside. Stack broccoli stems horizontally in feed tube and slice using firm pressure.

Add red and green pepper, zucchini and broccoli stems to skillet and cook over medium heat until vegetables are tender but not limp, about 10 to 12 minutes. While vegetables are cooking, bring large saucepan of salted water to boil over high heat. Add broccoli florets and blanch 30 seconds. Immediately plunge florets into cold water to stop cooking process. Drain well.

Using French fry disc, process tomatoes using light pressure. Drain tomato pieces well, discarding juice. Add tomato pieces, reserved parsley, Sherry vinegar, broccoli florets, salt, oregano and nutmeg to vegetables in skillet. Toss gently to blend. *(Can be prepared several hours ahead to this point.)*

Combine water and salt in large pot and bring to boil over high heat. Add pasta. After water returns to boil, cook pasta until al dente, about 30 seconds. Drain pasta thoroughly.

Just before serving, place remaining 3 tablespoons butter in heated shallow large serving dish. Add hot drained pasta, 1¼ cups Parmesan, half of Romano and freshly ground white pepper and toss gently. Top with vegetable mixture. Sprinkle with remaining Parmesan and Romano and pepper.

Vegetable Pasta

3 to 4 servings

- **3 tablespoons olive oil**
- **3 garlic cloves, minced**
- **¼ cup chopped onion**
- **1 pint cherry tomatoes, halved**
- **2 cups chopped broccoli, cooked until crisp-tender and drained**
- **1 tablespoon chopped fresh basil or ½ teaspoon dried, crumbled**
- **½ teaspoon crushed red pepper flakes or to taste**
- **Salt and freshly ground pepper**
- **8 ounces fettuccine, freshly cooked and drained**
- **Freshly grated Parmesan cheese**

Heat oil in large skillet over medium-high heat. Add garlic and onion and sauté until tender, about 5 to 10 minutes. Add tomatoes and cook until softened, about 10 minutes. Blend in broccoli and seasonings. Add fettuccine and toss lightly. Sprinkle lightly with Parmesan and toss again. Pass additional cheese at table.

Green Tomato Spaghetti with Red Tomato Sauce (Spaghetti alla Prematura)

A very light, summery pasta dish.

6 servings

Pasta

- **1 medium-size green tomato, seeded**
- **2½ cups unbleached all purpose flour**
- **2 extra-large eggs**
- **2 teaspoons olive oil**
- **Pinch of salt**

Sauce

- **1 tablespoon butter**
- **¼ cup olive oil**
- **1 medium garlic clove**
- **1 pound fresh Italian plum tomatoes, seeded and coarsely chopped**
- **Salt and freshly ground pepper**
- **5 Italian parsley sprigs**
- **3 fresh basil leaves**

- **½ cup (1 stick) butter, room temperature**

For pasta: Puree green tomato in processor or pass through food mill. Strain through fine sieve into small bowl. Arrange flour in mound on work surface and make well in center. Blend pureed tomato, eggs, oil and salt in well with fork. Gradually draw flour from inner edge of well into center until half of flour is incorporated. Gather dough together. Scrape work surface with pastry scraper, gathering all unincorporated flour, and place in sifter set over work surface. Sift flour to remove hard dough pieces; discard pieces. Knead dough on sifted flour until smooth, about 3 minutes.

Cut pasta into 6 to 8 pieces. Flatten 1 piece of dough (keep remainder covered). Turn machine to widest setting and run dough through. Dust dough with flour if sticky and fold into thirds. Run dough through machine 8 to 10 times until smooth and velvety, folding dough before each run. Adjust pasta machine to next narrower setting. Run dough through machine, dusting lightly with flour if necessary. Repeat, narrowing rollers after each run until pasta is ⅛ inch thick. Cut dough sheet into 15-inch-long pieces. Set on lightly floured kitchen towels. Repeat with remaining dough. Set aside until sheets look firm and leathery and edges begin to curl, 10 to 30 minutes depending on dampness of dough. *Pasta must be cut at this point or dough will be too brittle.*

Run dough sheets through narrowest blades of pasta machine or cut into spaghetti by hand. Arrange pasta on lightly floured surface, overlapping as little as possible. Cover with towel and set aside until ready to cook.

For sauce: Melt 1 tablespoon butter with oil in heavy small saucepan over medium heat. Add garlic and sauté until lightly colored, about 5 minutes. Discard garlic. Stir tomatoes into pan. Reduce heat, cover and simmer until tomatoes are soft, about 15 minutes, stirring occasionally. Season with salt and pepper. Mix in parsley and basil. Simmer 2 minutes to blend flavors. Pass sauce through fine disc of food mill into another heavy small saucepan. Keep warm over low heat.

Bring large amount of salted water to rapid boil in large pot. Place butter in large bowl and set atop pot of boiling water until butter melts. Remove bowl. Add pasta to water and stir vigorously to prevent sticking. Cook until light and tender, about 30 seconds if very fresh. Drain well. Toss pasta with butter. Spoon sauce over pasta and toss. Serve immediately.

Pasta del Sol

Use whatever green vegetables are the freshest and the best, and supplement with frozen vegetables if you like. Use equal amounts (approximately 1½ cups) of all vegetables except peas, Chinese pea pods and red pepper.

6 to 8 appetizer servings

1½ cups green beans, trimmed and cut into 1¼-inch lengths
2 unpeeled medium zucchini, cut lengthwise into sixths and cut into 1¼-inch lengths, or 4 unpeeled small zucchini, quartered lengthwise and cut into 1¼-inch lengths (about 1½ cups)
1½ cups very small broccoli florets
1½ cups chopped asparagus (cut about 1 to 1¼ inches long)
1½ cups green bell pepper julienne (cut 1¼ inches long)
1 cup red bell pepper julienne (cut 1¼ inches long)
¾ cup fresh peas or frozen tiny peas
¾ cup fresh or frozen snow peas (as small as possible)

3 tablespoons (or more) olive oil
¼ cup chopped green onion
1 teaspoon finely chopped garlic
½ cup coarsely chopped Italian parsley or ½ cup minced curly-leaf parsley
1 teaspoon finely chopped fresh green chilies or scant ½ teaspoon crushed dried red chili
Salt and freshly ground pepper
½ cup (about) coarsely chopped fresh basil or 2 teaspoons dried, crumbled

¼ cup (½ stick) butter
½ cup chicken stock
½ cup dry white wine

1 tablespoon olive or vegetable oil
1 teaspoon salt
1 pound fettuccine or spaghetti, preferably fresh

⅔ cup freshly grated Parmesan cheese
½ cup toasted pine nuts
Additional chicken stock (optional)
Freshly grated Parmesan cheese

Blanch each of the vegetables separately in rapidly boiling salted water until just tender, about 2 to 3 minutes per vegetable (peas will take only 1 minute if fresh or 30 seconds or less if frozen). Drain each vegetable well after cooking. Refresh in cold water and drain again; pat dry if necessary. Combine all vegetables in large bowl and set aside.

Heat 3 tablespoons olive oil in large skillet over medium heat. Add green onion and garlic and sauté about 3 minutes; *do not brown.* Add parsley, chilies and salt and pepper to taste and sauté an additional 2 minutes. Blend in basil.

Add more oil to skillet if necessary. Add vegetables and stir gently to heat through, 1 to 2 minutes. Set aside.

For sauce, melt butter in Dutch oven or large deep skillet (large enough to accommodate pasta and vegetables) over low heat. Stir in stock and wine and bring to simmer. Cover and set aside.

Bring large quantity of water to boil with 1 tablespoon oil and 1 teaspoon salt. Add pasta and stir with wooden spoon to separate. Cook until pasta is al dente (firm to the bite).

Reheat sauce if necessary. Add pasta and half of vegetable mixture and toss gently to mix. Add remaining vegetables with 2/3 cup Parmesan and pine nuts and toss again. Add more stock if mixture seems too dry (sauce should not be soupy). Divide among heated plates and serve immediately, passing additional grated Parmesan at table.

Pansotti with Pesto, Tomatoes and Cream (Pansotti con Pesto, Pomodoro e Panna)

A variation of the classic dish that originated around Genoa in Liguria.

4 servings

Filling

- 1 1/2 pounds fresh spinach, stemmed (about 1 1/2 large bunches), or one 10-ounce package frozen spinach
- 1 cup water
- 1 teaspoon salt
- 3 tablespoons butter
- 1 garlic clove, finely chopped
- 1/3 cup (or more) freshly grated Parmesan cheese
- 4 ounces ricotta cheese
- Salt and freshly ground pepper

Pansotti

- 2 cups all purpose flour, preferably unbleached
- 3 eggs, room temperature

Pesto Sauce

- 3 cups loosely packed fresh basil leaves
- 3/4 cup olive oil
- 1/4 cup toasted pine nuts (about 1 ounce)
- 1 teaspoon salt
- 3 garlic cloves
- 1/2 cup freshly grated Parmesan cheese
- 3 tablespoons freshly grated Romano or Parmesan cheese

- 3 to 4 tablespoons butter
- 2 tomatoes, peeled, cored, seeded and finely chopped
- 1/3 cup whipping cream

- 1 tablespoon olive or vegetable oil

- Butter
- 1 cup freshly grated Parmesan cheese

For filling: Combine spinach, water and salt in large pot or Dutch oven. Cover and bring to boil over high heat. Cook spinach until tender, about 2 to 3 minutes (if using frozen spinach, cook according to package directions). Drain spinach and squeeze dry. Melt butter in heavy saucepan over medium heat. Add garlic and cook 1 to 2 minutes. Stir in spinach and 1/3 cup Parmesan and cook until well mixed, about 2 minutes. Transfer mixture to processor or blender and mince using on/off turns. Add ricotta and mix just to blend (filling should retain some texture; if filling is too thin, add small amount of Parmesan). Taste and season with salt and pepper. Cover and refrigerate until ready to use.

For pansotti: Arrange flour in mound on work surface and make well in center. Break eggs into well and blend with fork. Gradually draw small amount of flour from inner edge of well into eggs with fork, stirring constantly until all flour is incorporated. Gather dough into loose mass and set aside. Scrape any hard bits of flour from work surface and discard. Lightly flour work surface and hands. Knead dough until smooth and elastic, 10 to 12 minutes. Insert finger in center of dough; if dry, dough is ready for pasta machine; if sticky, sprinkle dough lightly with flour and continue kneading until dough is correct consistency.

Cut off 1 egg-size piece of dough. Store remaining dough in plastic wrap or dry towel to prevent drying; set aside. Flatten piece of dough with heel of hand, then fold in half. Turn pasta machine to widest setting and run dough through. Continue folding and kneading process with pasta machine until dough is smooth and velvety, about 2 more times (number will depend on how vigorously dough was kneaded by hand). Dust dough lightly with more flour as necessary.

Adjust pasta machine to next narrower setting. Run dough through machine *without folding,* dusting lightly with flour if sticky. Repeat, narrowing rollers after each run until machine is on second to narrowest setting; pasta should be less than 1/16 inch thick.

To shape pansotti, immediately trim dough sheet to width of 3 inches. Cut dough into 3-inch triangles using pastry wheel. Arrange 1 heaping teaspoon filling in center of triangle. Fold triangle over to form another triangle half as large, pressing edges to seal. Transfer pansotti to kitchen towel set on baking sheet; do not let pansotti overlap. Repeat with remaining dough. *(Can be prepared ahead to this point. Cover with kitchen towel and chill until ready to use.)*

For sauce: Combine basil, 3/4 cup oil, pine nuts, salt and garlic in processor or blender and mix until smooth. Transfer to small bowl. Stir in 1/2 cup Parmesan and 3 tablespoons Romano. Taste and season with salt and pepper.

Melt 3 to 4 tablespoons butter in large skillet over medium-high heat. Add tomato and cook until liquid evaporates, about 2 to 3 minutes. Stir in basil mixture and cream. Reduce heat to low and cook, stirring constantly, until sauce is thick and creamy. Season with salt and pepper. Set aside.

Meanwhile, fill pasta cooker or stockpot 3/4 full with salted water and bring to rapid boil over high heat. Stir in 1 tablespoon oil. Add pansotti and stir vigorously to prevent sticking. Cook until just firm but tender to bite (al dente); taste often to prevent overcooking. Drain.

Butter heated serving platter. Transfer pansotti to platter. Place sauce over medium-high heat and stir until heated through. Pour sauce over pasta and toss gently until pasta is well coated. Serve immediately. Pass remaining grated Parmesan cheese separately.

Green and Red Pepper Lasagne (Lasagne di Peperoni)

This recipe is from Giuliano Bugialli, the famed Tuscan cooking teacher. He cuts the pasta dough into five pieces before rolling it out into very long strips. Less experienced cooks will find it easier to cut the dough into eight to 10 pieces.

8 to 10 servings

Pasta

2 medium-size green bell peppers, seeded and coarsely chopped
2 medium garlic cloves
5 1/4 cups unbleached all purpose flour
3 extra-large eggs
1 tablespoon olive oil
Pinch of salt
Freshly ground pepper

2 tablespoons olive oil

Red Bell Pepper Tomato Sauce

3/4 cup olive oil
3 large red bell peppers, seeded and coarsely chopped
3 medium garlic cloves
3 pounds fresh Italian plum tomatoes, quartered, or 4 cups canned (undrained)
15 Italian parsley sprigs (leaves only), coarsely chopped
Salt and freshly ground pepper

Béchamel Sauce

1/2 cup (1 stick) unsalted butter
1/2 cup unbleached all purpose flour
3 1/2 cups milk, scalded
Salt and freshly ground pepper

1 cup freshly grated Parmesan cheese, preferably imported

For pasta: Finely grind peppers and garlic in processor or blender. Measure 3/4 cup to use in pasta. Arrange flour in mound on work surface and make well in center. Blend pepper mixture, eggs, 1 tablespoon olive oil, salt and pepper in well with fork. Gradually draw flour from inner edge of well into center until half of flour is incorporated. Gather dough together. Scrape work surface with pastry scraper, gathering all unincorporated flour, and place in sifter set over work surface. Sift flour to remove hard dough pieces; discard pieces. Knead dough on sifted flour until smooth, about 3 minutes.

Cut pasta into 8 to 10 pieces. Flatten 1 piece of dough (keep remainder covered). Turn pasta machine to widest setting and run dough through. Dust dough with flour if sticky and fold into thirds. Run through machine 8 to 10 more times until smooth, flouring and folding before each run.

Adjust pasta machine to next narrower setting. Run dough through machine, dusting lightly with flour if necessary. Repeat, narrowing rollers after each run until dough is 1/16 inch thick. Set on lightly floured surface. Repeat with remaining dough. Cut pasta into 6-inch-long pieces, using pastry cutter or knife. Let dry 10 minutes in single layer on floured surface.

Bring large amount of salted water to rapid boil in large pot. Fill large bowl 3/4 full with cold water; add 2 tablespoons olive oil. Add 3 pasta squares to boiling water. Return water to boil, then cook pasta 5 seconds. Transfer pasta to bowl of cold water to cool, using slotted spoon. Set in single layer on dampened towels. Repeat with remaining pasta. Let rest at least 20 minutes. *(Can be prepared 2 hours ahead.)*

For sauce: Heat oil in heavy large saucepan over medium heat. Add peppers and whole garlic and cook 5 minutes. Stir in tomatoes and parsley. Cover and simmer 25 minutes, stirring occasionally. Add salt and pepper to taste. Pass sauce through food mill into large bowl, then strain through fine sieve back into saucepan. Simmer until sauce is thick and smooth, about 15 minutes. Adjust seasoning. Transfer sauce to bowl. Cool completely.

For béchamel: Melt butter in heavy medium saucepan over low heat until bubbling. Mix in flour. Remove from heat 15 seconds. Return to low heat and add hot milk all at once, stirring until smooth. Bring to boil, reduce heat and simmer 10 minutes, stirring constantly. Season with salt and pepper. Pour into large bowl. Press sheet of buttered waxed paper onto surface of sauce to prevent skin from forming. Cool to room temperature.

To assemble, butter 8 3/4 × 13 1/2-inch baking dish. Arrange single layer of pasta squares in dish, allowing 1 inch to hang over edges. Spread 1/3 of béchamel over pasta in bottom of dish. Sprinkle with 1/3 cup Parmesan. Cover with another layer of pasta. Spoon on 1/4 cup pepper tomato sauce. Repeat pasta and pepper tomato sauce layers 3 more times. Add another layer of pasta, then another 1/3 of béchamel sauce and 1/3 cup Parmesan. Make 4 more layers *each* of pasta and remaining pepper tomato sauce. Top with another layer of pasta. Cover with remaining béchamel and Parmesan. Cover with final layer of pasta. Fold edges in over top layer. *(Can be prepared 1 day ahead and refrigerated. Bring to room temperature before continuing.)*

Preheat oven to 375°F. Bake lasagne until top is light golden brown and crisp, about 25 minutes. Let cool for 5 minutes before serving.

Whole Wheat Herb Pasta

2 to 4 servings

5 tablespoons butter
1/4 cup minced fresh parsley
1 teaspoon dried oregano, crumbled
1 teaspoon dried rosemary, crumbled
1 small garlic clove, minced
4 ounces mushrooms, sliced
8 ounces whole wheat spaghetti, freshly cooked and drained
3 tablespoons freshly grated Parmesan cheese

Melt 4 tablespoons butter in heavy skillet over low heat. Add parsley, oregano, rosemary and garlic and blend well. Remove from heat and let steep. Meanwhile, melt remaining 1 tablespoon butter in another skillet over low heat. Add mushrooms and sauté over medium-high heat until tender, about 4 minutes. Transfer to large serving dish. Add spaghetti, reserved herb butter and Parmesan cheese and toss gently. Serve immediately.

Minestrone Soup

6 to 8 servings

1/4 cup dried pinto beans

1 slice bacon, diced
1 cup diced zucchini
1/2 cup diced peeled eggplant
1/2 cup chopped leek
1/2 cup chopped fennel
1/4 cup chopped onion
1/4 cup diced celery
2 tablespoons diced carrot
1 3/4 quarts (7 cups) beef or chicken stock
1/2 cup dry white wine
1 large tomato, peeled, seeded and chopped
1/2 cup diced peeled potato
1/2 teaspoon tomato paste
1/2 cup cooked pasta

1/4 cup chopped fresh parsley
1/2 bunch fresh basil (leaves only)
2 garlic cloves
Pinch of dried oregano, crumbled
Salt and freshly ground pepper

Soak pinto beans in cold water to cover at least 3 hours or overnight.

Drain beans well. Transfer to small saucepan. Cover with cold water. Bring to boil over medium-high heat. Reduce heat and simmer until tender. Drain and set aside.

Sauté bacon briefly in Dutch oven over medium-high heat. Add zucchini, eggplant, leek, fennel, onion, celery and carrot and sauté until vegetables are slightly softened. Stir in stock, wine, tomato, potato and tomato paste and bring to boil. Reduce heat and simmer 30 minutes. Add beans and pasta and cook until heated through.

Mash together parsley, basil, garlic and oregano in small bowl. Add to soup a little at a time, tasting after each addition. Season with salt and pepper. Ladle soup into bowls and serve immediately.

Cream of Vegetable Soup with Mushrooms and Maltagliati (Passato di Verdura con Funghi e Maltagliati)

6 to 8 servings

Maltagliati

- ¾ cup all purpose flour, preferably unbleached
- 1 egg, room temperature

Soup

- ¼ cup olive oil
- 1 medium onion, finely chopped
- 2 tablespoons chopped fresh parsley
- 2 medium garlic cloves, minced
- 4 ounces asparagus, thinly sliced
- 4 ounces green beans, thinly sliced
- ¾ cup fresh peas (about 12 ounces unshelled)
- 1 potato, peeled and diced
- 1 large zucchini, diced
- 1 medium carrot, diced
- 1 tablespoon all purpose flour
- 1 tablespoon tomato paste
- 10 to 12 cups homemade beef broth or 5 to 6 cups canned mixed with 5 to 6 cups water
- Salt and freshly ground pepper

- 2 tablespoons (¼ stick) butter
- 4 ounces mushrooms, thinly sliced
- ⅓ cup whipping cream

- 1 tablespoon olive or vegetable oil

- 1 cup freshly grated Parmesan cheese

For maltagliati: Arrange flour in mound on work surface and make well in center. Break eggs into well and blend with fork. Gradually draw small amount of flour from inner edge of well into eggs with fork, stirring constantly until all flour is incorporated. Gather dough into loose mass and set aside. Scrape any hard bits of flour from work surface and discard. Lightly flour work surface and hands. Knead dough until smooth and elastic, 10 to 12 minutes. Insert finger in center of dough; if dry, dough is ready for pasta machine; if sticky, sprinkle dough lightly with flour and continue kneading until dough is correct consistency.

Cut off 1 egg-size piece of dough. Store remaining dough in plastic wrap or dry towel to prevent drying; set aside. Flatten piece of dough with heel of hand, then fold in half. Turn pasta machine to widest setting and run dough through. Continue folding and kneading process with pasta machine until dough is smooth and velvety, about 2 more times (number will depend on how vigorously dough was kneaded by hand). Dust dough lightly with more flour as necessary.

Adjust pasta machine to next narrower setting. Run dough through machine *without folding,* dusting lightly with flour if sticky. Repeat, narrowing rollers after each run until machine is on second to narrowest setting; pasta should be less than 1/16 inch thick.

Knead and shape remaining dough into sheets, kneading each egg-size piece of dough slightly before running through machine. Set aside until sheets look firm and leathery and edges begin to curl up slightly but are not brittle. This will take 10 to 30 minutes depending on dryness of dough and temperature and humidity of kitchen. *Pasta must be cut at this point or dough will be too brittle.*

To shape maltagliati, fold over short end of 1 dough sheet about 3 inches. Continue folding dough over to form 3-inch-wide rectangle. Cut both corners off 1 short end of rectangle to form 2 narrow irregular triangles about 1½ inches long across base. Then, cut resulting point off (folded dough will be rectangular again). Continue cutting process until entire length of folded dough is used. Transfer maltagliati to kitchen towel set on baking sheet. Repeat with remaining dough sheets. *(Can be left overnight to dry completely in cool dry place.)*

For soup: Heat oil in large pot or Dutch oven over medium-low heat. Add onion, parsley and garlic. Cover and cook until onion is golden, about 10 minutes. Mix in asparagus, beans, peas, potato, zucchini and carrot and cook 2 to 3 minutes. Add flour and cook 3 minutes, stirring constantly. Dilute tomato paste in small amount of broth. Blend into vegetable mixture. Add remaining broth. Taste and season with salt and pepper. Increase heat to high and bring to boil. Reduce heat to low, cover and cook for 1 hour.

Transfer vegetables and broth to processor or blender in batches and mix until smooth. Strain mixture back into saucepan. Melt butter in medium skillet over high heat. Add mushrooms and sauté until lightly golden. Season with salt and pepper to taste. Add mushrooms to soup mixture. Stir in cream. Keep soup warm over low heat.

Meanwhile, fill pasta cooker or stockpot 3/4 full with salted water and bring to rapid boil over high heat. Stir in 1 tablespoon oil. Add maltagliati and stir vigorously to prevent sticking. Cook until just firm but tender to bite (al dente), about 5 to 20 seconds for freshly made and up to 3 minutes for thoroughly dried pasta. Taste often to prevent overcooking. Drain.

Stir pasta into soup. Ladle into bowls and serve. Pass cheese separately.

4 *Pasta with Seafood*

For sheer elegance there is nothing to compare with choice fish and shellfish; any meal that includes a delicacy like scallops, lobster or smoked salmon is sure to be extraordinary. In this chapter you will find dishes—some simple, some elaborate—that elevate any meal to the realm of the truly memorable.

When a seafood sauce is paired with just the right homemade pasta the result can be dazzling: Among such showstoppers are Lemon Tagliolini with Fresh Clam Sauce (page 57), Red Pepper Pasta with Lobster and Basil (page 59), Chive-Lemon Tortelli Filled with Scallop Mousse (page 62) and Shrimp and Feta with Rice Flour Pasta (page 64). But other recipes prove that quickly-prepared sauces teamed with store-bought pasta can also be sensationally good—consider Linguine with New England Clam Sauce (page 56), Crab and Pasta Genovese (page 58) and Calistoga Inn's Fettuccine with Smoked Salmon (page 60).

As with all fish and shellfish recipes, the cardinal rule here is not to overcook. Since the seafood itself only cooks for a few minutes, most of the sauces in this section are correspondingly quick to prepare. They are proof positive that wonderful food does not have to mean long hours in the kitchen.

Fusilli Pugliesi

4 servings

1 cup extra virgin olive oil
1 2-ounce can anchovy fillets packed in olive oil, drained and chopped
4 garlic cloves, minced
Dried red pepper flakes

1 pound spinach fusilli

8 ounces broccoli, cut into florets (stems discarded)

1 teaspoon minced fresh parsley
6 tablespoons freshly grated Parmesan cheese

Combine oil, anchovies and garlic in heavy small skillet. Add red pepper flakes to taste. Set oil mixture aside.

Cook fusilli in rapidly boiling salted water until just tender but firm to bite. Cook broccoli florets in another pot of rapidly boiling salted water until crisp-tender; do not overcook.

Meanwhile, place oil mixture over low heat. Add parsley and heat through. Drain fusilli and broccoli. Transfer to medium bowl. Add oil mixture and toss well. Add cheese and toss again. Serve immediately.

Linguine with New England Clam Sauce

4 servings

1/4 cup (1/2 stick) butter
1 1/2 cups minced onion
1/2 cup diced carrot
1/2 cup diced celery
1/2 cup diced green bell pepper
3 tablespoons all purpose flour
2 cups fish or chicken stock
1/2 cup dry white wine
1/2 teaspoon dried thyme, crumbled
1/4 teaspoon freshly ground pepper
3 dozen littleneck clams, scrubbed

1 pound linguine or spaghetti
1/4 cup (1/2 stick) butter

Salt
1/4 cup minced fresh parsley

Melt 1/4 cup butter in large skillet over medium-low heat. Add vegetables, cover and cook until mixture begins to soften, about 5 minutes. Sprinkle with flour and stir 3 minutes. Mix in stock, wine, thyme and pepper. Boil until sauce thickens, stirring constantly, about 5 minutes. Add clams. Cover and steam 5 minutes. Remove opened clams. Cover and continue cooking remaining clams about 5 minutes longer; discard any that do not open.

Remove 24 clams from shells; return to skillet. Keep sauce warm.

Cook pasta in large pot of boiling salted water until just tender but firm to bite. Drain well. Transfer to large bowl. Mix in 1/4 cup butter.

Season sauce with salt. Pour over pasta. Add parsley and toss to blend. Divide among heated shallow bowls. Garnish with remaining clams (in shells). Serve immediately.

Salsa Piccante with fusilli

Irwin Horowitz

Pasta

Clockwise from top right: small squares of Saffron Pasta; Broccoli Fettuccine; Carrot Fettuccine; Lemon Tagliolini; Orange Pappardelle; Green Pea Farfalle

Rudi Legname

Fresh Basil Pesto with fettuccine

Brian Leatart

Irwin Horowitz

Pasta Timbale with Chianti Vinaigrette

Dan Wolfe

Clockwise from top right: Pesto Sauce; Mediterranean Sauce; Tomato and Mozzarella Sauce

Vegetable Fettuccine Carbonara

Dick Sharpe

Lemon Tagliolini with Fresh Clam Sauce

4 servings

3 dozen small clams in shell
2/3 cup dry white wine or dry vermouth

1/4 cup olive oil
2 tablespoons (1/4 stick) unsalted butter
2 teaspoons minced shallot
2 garlic cloves, minced
2 teaspoons minced fresh parsley
1 teaspoon fresh oregano or 1/2 teaspoon dried, crumbled
1/4 teaspoon dried red pepper flakes or to taste

1 tablespoon olive or vegetable oil
1/2 recipe Lemon Tagliolini (see page 5)
1/4 cup freshly grated Parmesan cheese (optional)
Salt
1 tablespoon minced lemon peel

Combine clams and 1/3 cup wine in large saucepan over medium-high heat. Cover and boil until clams open, about 5 minutes. Remove opened clams using slotted spoon. Continue cooking until remaining clams open, about 5 minutes. Discard any clams that do not open. When cool enough to handle, remove clams from shells. Strain clam broth through several thicknesses of dampened cheesecloth. Return to pan and boil until reduced to 3/4 cup. Remove from heat.

Heat oil and butter in heavy medium saucepan over medium-low heat. Add shallot and garlic and sauté until shallot is translucent. Add remaining 1/3 cup wine, strained clam broth, parsley, oregano and red pepper flakes. Reduce heat to low and simmer until reduced slightly, about 10 minutes. Add clams; remove saucepan from heat.

Bring large amount of salted water to rapid boil in large pot. Stir in 1 tablespoon oil. Add pasta and stir vigorously to prevent sticking. Cook until just firm but almost tender to the bite (al dente), about 2 minutes. Drain well. Warm sauce over high heat. Toss with pasta. Add cheese if desired and toss again. Season with salt. Sprinkle with lemon peel and serve.

King Crab Fettuccine

4 to 6 servings

1/2 cup (1 stick) butter
1 garlic clove, minced
8 ounces fresh or frozen Alaskan king crabmeat, drained and separated into chunks
3/4 cup whipping cream
1/2 cup freshly grated Parmesan cheese
1/2 teaspoon coarsely ground pepper
Salt
12 ounces fettuccine, freshly cooked and drained
1 tablespoon chopped fresh parsley

Melt butter in heavy medium skillet over medium heat. Add garlic and sauté until golden. Stir in crabmeat, cream, Parmesan, pepper and salt and stir until well blended. Pour crab sauce over fettuccine in large serving bowl and toss well. Sprinkle with fresh parsley and serve immediately.

Crab and Pasta Genovese

4 servings

- ½ cup vegetable oil
- ½ cup chopped onion
- 2 garlic cloves, minced
- ½ cup chopped black olives
- ¼ cup chopped fresh parsley
- 2 tablespoons chopped red or green bell pepper
- 2 teaspoons fresh lemon juice
- ½ teaspoon dried basil, crumbled
- ¼ teaspoon dried oregano, crumbled
- 8 ounces cooked crab, drained and shredded
- ½ cup chopped walnuts
- 8 ounces freshly cooked spaghetti or linguine
- Salt and freshly ground pepper

Heat oil in large skillet over medium heat. Add onion and garlic and sauté until onion is translucent. Add olives, parsley, bell pepper, lemon juice, basil and oregano and cook 2 minutes, stirring frequently. Add crab and cook 3 more minutes. Mix in walnuts. Transfer to serving bowl. Add pasta and toss to combine. Season with salt and pepper. Serve immediately.

Fresh Tomato Soup with Spinach Ravioli

10 servings

Tomato Soup

- ¼ cup olive oil
- 6½ pounds tomatoes (about 16 medium), peeled, seeded and crushed
- 2 medium onions, chopped
- 2 celery stalks, chopped

- 1 tablespoon butter
- 1 tablespoon all purpose flour
- 3¾ cups chicken stock
- 3 tablespoons tomato paste
- 1 tablespoon sugar
- 1 tablespoon paprika
- Salt and freshly ground pepper

Crab Filling

- 8 ounces cooked crabmeat, shredded
- 2 tablespoons mayonnaise
- 1 tablespoon capers, rinsed and drained
- 2 teaspoons snipped fresh chives
- 1½ teaspoons Worcestershire sauce
- 1½ teaspoons fresh lemon juice
- ⅛ teaspoon dried dillweed
- Pinch of freshly ground white pepper

Spinach Pasta

- 8 ounces fresh spinach, stemmed, or ½ 10-ounce package frozen spinach, prepared according to package instructions, squeezed dry

- ½ cup all purpose flour
- 1 egg, room temperature
- 1 egg yolk, room temperature
- 1 teaspoon olive oil
- 1 teaspoon fresh lemon juice
- ½ teaspoon freshly grated nutmeg
- Pinch of salt

For soup: Heat oil in heavy stockpot over medium heat. Add tomatoes, onions and celery. Cover and simmer until tomatoes are very tender, about 25 minutes. Puree mixture in processor.

Melt butter in heavy large saucepan over medium-low heat. Add flour and whisk in corner of pan 3 minutes. Whisk in stock. Increase heat to medium-high and stir until mixture comes to boil. Add reserved tomato mixture, tomato paste, sugar and paprika. Continue cooking soup until reduced to desired thickness. Season with salt and pepper. *(Can be prepared 2 days ahead and refrigerated or frozen for longer period. Reheat before serving.)*

For filling: Mix crab, mayonnaise, capers, chives, Worcestershire, lemon juice, dillweed, salt and pepper in large bowl. Cover and refrigerate. *(Filling can be prepared 1 day ahead.)*

For pasta: Stir spinach over medium-high heat in heavy large skillet until wilted and cooked, about 3 minutes. Cool. Squeeze dry. Puree in processor.

Add 6 tablespoons flour with egg, egg yolk, oil, lemon juice, nutmeg and salt to spinach and process. Mix in remaining flour 1 tablespoon at a time until dough leaves sides of work bowl but is still soft. Process until smooth, about 40 seconds. Turn dough out onto lightly floured surface and knead 1 to 2 minutes. *(Dough can also be prepared by hand.)* Wrap in plastic and let rest 1 hour at room temperature.

Divide dough into 4 pieces. Wrap 3 pieces in plastic to prevent drying. Pat remaining piece of dough into 4 × 6-inch rectangle. Turn pasta machine to widest setting. Fold rectangle into thirds and run dough through machine. Continue folding and kneading process with pasta machine until dough is smooth and velvety, about 10 more times. Dust dough lightly with more flour as necessary.

Adjust pasta machine to next narrower setting. Run dough through machine *without folding,* dusting lightly with flour if sticky. Repeat, narrowing rollers after each run until machine is on second narrowest setting; pasta should be less than 1/16 inch thick.

Cut dough strip crosswise in half. Lay 1 piece loosely over lightly floured 1½-inch ravioli mold. Gently press dough into molds; if dough tears, patch with small piece of dough and seal with dab of water. Fill each pocket with generous ½ teaspoon filling. Using small brush or fingertip, moisten rim of dough with water. Cover with second dough strip half, pressing unfilled dough from center outward to remove any air pockets. Press around edge of dough to seal. Run rolling pin or back of spoon down seams of mold to seal and cut ravioli. Arrange in single layer on lightly floured towel. Repeat with remaining dough and filling. *(Ravioli can be prepared 1 day ahead. Cover ravioli with kitchen towel and refrigerate until ready to cook.)*

To serve, reheat soup if necessary. Bring covered stockpot of salted water to rapid boil over high heat. Add ravioli (in batches of no more than 18) and stir to prevent sticking. Cook uncovered until pasta is just firm but tender to the bite (al dente), about 5 to 6 minutes. Drain well. Ladle hot soup into individual bowls. Divide ravioli among bowls. Serve immediately.

Red Pepper Pasta with Lobster and Basil

4 first-course servings

7 cups water
2 1½-pound lobsters, boiled, shelled (shells reserved) and tail meat cut into ¼-inch-thick medallions
1 cup plus 10 tablespoons California Chardonnay
½ cup minced shallot
½ bunch parsley
5 thyme sprigs or ½ teaspoon dried, crumbled
1 bay leaf
3 peppercorns

2 cups whipping cream
Salt

2 tablespoons olive oil
12 ounces Red Pepper Pasta*

½ cup thinly sliced fresh basil leaves

Combine water, lobster shells, wine, shallot, parsley, thyme, bay leaf and peppercorns in large pot. Simmer 20 minutes. Strain liquid into heavy large saucepan. Boil until reduced to ½ cup, about 45 minutes. *(Can be prepared 8 hours ahead. Cover and refrigerate.)*

Add cream to liquid and boil until consistency of whipping cream, about 6 minutes. Taste and season with salt.

Meanwhile, bring large amount of salted water to rapid boil in large pot. Add 2 tablespoons oil. Stir in pasta. Cook until just tender but firm to bite, about 20 seconds. Drain well.

Add lobster medallions to sauce and quickly heat through. Remove using slotted spoon. Add pasta to sauce and stir until coated. Transfer to heated platter. Top with lobster and basil.

*Red Pepper Pasta

Makes about 1½ pounds

1¼ pounds red bell peppers

3 cups (about) all purpose flour
6 egg yolks

Preheat oven to 375°F. Char peppers over gas flame or under broiler, turning occasionally, until skin blackens. Place on baking sheet and roast until tender, about 15 minutes. Wrap in plastic bag and let stand 10 minutes to steam. Peel and seed peppers, rinsing if necessary. Pat dry. Puree in blender or processor.

Arrange 2¾ cups flour in mound in large bowl and make well in center. Add pepper puree and yolks to well and blend with fork. Gradually draw flour from inner edge of well into center until all flour is incorporated. Knead dough on lightly floured surface until smooth, about 8 minutes, kneading in more flour if sticky. Cover and let rest at least 30 minutes.

Cut dough into 12 pieces. Flatten 1 piece of dough (keep remainder covered), then fold in thirds and dust with flour if sticky. Turn pasta machine to widest setting and run dough through until smooth and velvety, about 6 times, folding before each run. Adjust pasta machine to next narrower setting. Run dough through machine without folding. Repeat, narrowing rollers after each run, until pasta is 1/16 inch thick, dusting with flour as necessary. Hang dough sheet on drying rack or place on kitchen towels. Repeat with remaining dough. Set aside until sheets look leathery and edges begin to curl, 10 to 30 minutes. *Pasta must be cut at this point or dough sheets will be too brittle.*

Run sheets through finest cutting blades of pasta machine (or cut by hand into fine strands). Arrange pasta on drying rack or kitchen towel, overlapping as little as possible, until ready to cook. *(Pasta can be frozen.)*

Calistoga Inn's Fettuccine with Smoked Salmon

4 main-course or 6 first-course servings

4 cups whipping cream
½ cup (1 stick) butter
12 ounces smoked salmon, cut into julienne
¼ cup minced fresh chives
Freshly ground pepper
1 pound fettuccine, freshly cooked and drained
Parsley sprigs (garnish)

Combine cream and butter in medium saucepan and cook over medium-high heat until thick, glossy and reduced by half. Add salmon, chives and pepper and cook, stirring gently, about 1 minute. Transfer fettuccine to serving platter. Pour sauce over and toss just to blend. Garnish with parsley and serve.

Spaghetti with Smoked Salmon

6 servings

- 1/4 cup olive oil
- 2 garlic cloves, minced
- 4 ounces smoked Nova Scotia salmon, cut crosswise into thin strips
- 1 4 1/4-ounce can chopped olives, drained
- 1 cup whipping cream
- 8 ounces tomatoes, peeled, seeded and pureed
- 1/2 to 1 teaspoon dried mint, crumbled
- 1/2 to 1 teaspoon dried oregano, crumbled
- Salt
- 1 pound spaghetti, freshly cooked and drained

Heat oil in medium skillet over medium-high heat. Add garlic and sauté until softened. Add salmon and olives and cook, stirring frequently, about 2 minutes. Blend in cream and stir until thickened. Mix in tomatoes. Reduce heat and season with mint, oregano and salt. Cook about 5 minutes. Spoon over pasta and serve.

Carrot Fettuccine with Carrots, Scallops and Vermouth

4 to 6 servings

- 8 ounces carrots, peeled and cut into matchstick julienne
- 1/2 cup dry vermouth
- 1/3 cup olive oil
- 1 1/2 teaspoons fresh marjoram or 1/2 teaspoon dried, crumbled
- 1 1/2 teaspoons fresh thyme or 1/2 teaspoon dried, crumbled
- 1 teaspoon salt
- 1 small bay leaf
- 1/2 teaspoon coriander seed, crushed
- 1/4 teaspoon minced garlic
- Pinch of dried red pepper flakes
- 8 ounces onions, thinly sliced

- 1 pound whole bay scallops or quartered sea scallops
- 1/4 cup fresh lemon juice
- 1/4 cup chopped fresh parsley
- 2 tablespoons snipped fresh chives
- Freshly ground pepper

- 2 tablespoons olive oil
- Carrot Fettuccine*

Combine carrots, vermouth, 1/3 cup oil, marjoram, thyme, salt, bay leaf, coriander, garlic and red pepper flakes in large saucepan and bring to simmer. Cover and cook 5 minutes. Add onions and simmer until carrots and onions are crisp-tender, about 5 more minutes. Transfer to nonaluminum bowl and let mixture cool to room temperature.

Stir scallops, lemon juice, parsley, chives and generous amount of pepper into carrot mixture. Cover and refrigerate until scallops turn completely opaque, 12 hours or overnight.

Bring large amount of salted water to rapid boil in large pot. Add 1 tablespoon olive oil. Add pasta and stir vigorously to prevent sticking. Cook until just firm but almost tender to the bite (al dente), about 3 minutes. Drain well. Toss with remaining 1 tablespoon olive oil. Cool. Discard bay leaf from scallops. Toss scallop mixture with pasta. Serve at room temperature.

*Carrot Fettuccine

Makes about 1 pound

- 3 large carrots, peeled and cut into 1-inch chunks

- 2 to 2 1/2 cups all purpose flour
- 3 to 4 tablespoons warm water
- 1 egg, room temperature
- 1 tablespoon olive oil
- 1 teaspoon salt

Cover carrots with water in medium saucepan and bring to simmer. Cook until very soft; drain. Puree in processor. Measure 2/3 cup to use in pasta.

Arrange 2 cups flour in mound on work surface or in large bowl and make well in center. Add 2/3 cup carrot puree, 3 tablespoons water, egg, oil and salt to well and blend with fork. Gradually draw flour from inner edge of well into center until all flour is incorporated. Add more water if necessary to bind dough. Lightly flour work surface and hands. Knead dough until smooth and elastic, about 15 minutes, kneading in some of remaining flour if necessary. Cover with inverted bowl or cloth; let rest at least 15 minutes.

Cut pasta dough into 4 pieces. Turn pasta machine to widest setting. Flatten 1 piece of dough (keep remainder covered to prevent drying), then fold in half or thirds and run through machine. Repeat until smooth and velvety (number of times will depend on how vigorously dough was kneaded by hand). Adjust machine to next narrower setting. Run dough through machine, dusting lightly with flour if sticky. Repeat, narrowing rollers until pasta is 1/16 inch thick. Hang dough sheet on drying rack or set on kitchen towels. Repeat with remaining dough. Dry sheets until firm and leathery and edges begin to curl slightly, but are not brittle, 10 to 30 minutes, depending on moistness of dough and temperature of kitchen. *Pasta must be cut at this point or dough will be too brittle.*

Run dough sheets through fettuccine blades of pasta machine (or cut by hand into strips about 1/4 inch wide). Arrange pasta on kitchen towel or drying rack, overlapping as little as possible. Set fettuccine aside until ready to cook.

Chive-Lemon Tortelli Filled with Scallop Mousse

Serve with spinach salad or arugula dressed with vinaigrette.

4 to 6 servings

Chive-Lemon Pasta

2 1/2 cups all purpose flour
1 teaspoon salt
3 egg yolks
3 eggs

2 tablespoons snipped fresh chives
1/2 teaspoon grated lemon peel

Scallop Mousse Filling

1 pound scallops
1 tablespoon minced shallot

2 egg whites, well chilled
1 cup whipping cream, well chilled
1 teaspoon salt
1/2 teaspoon freshly ground white pepper

1 egg blended with 1 tablespoon water

Chive Vinaigrette

1/2 cup Chive Vinegar*
2 tablespoons minced shallot
1 cup olive oil
1/2 teaspoon salt
Freshly ground pepper
2 tablespoons snipped fresh chives

For pasta: Mix flour and salt. Arrange flour in mound on work surface and make well in center. Add yolks and eggs to well and blend with fork. Gradually draw small amount of flour from inner edge of well into eggs with fork until all flour is incorporated. Blend in chives and lemon peel. Knead until smooth, several minutes. Divide dough into 4 pieces. Cover with towel and let rest 1 hour.

Meanwhile, prepare mousse: Combine scallops and shallot in processor and puree until smooth. Transfer mixture (in work bowl with steel knife and top intact) to refrigerator; chill 30 minutes.

Return work bowl to base. Add egg whites and mix 30 seconds. With machine running, pour cream through feed tube in slow steady stream and mix until thoroughly incorporated. Season mousse with salt and pepper. Refrigerate until ready to use. *(Can be prepared 3 hours ahead.)*

Fold 1 piece of dough in thirds and knead in pasta machine set at widest setting until smooth and velvety, about 10 times. Adjust pasta machine to next narrower setting. Run dough through machine without folding, narrowing rollers after each run until machine is on second to narrowest setting. Transfer pasta strip to towel-lined baking sheet. Cover with another towel to prevent drying. Repeat with remaining dough.

Immediately lay 1 pasta strip out on work surface. Arrange tablespoons of mousse lengthwise along bottom half of strip, spacing 2 inches apart. Brush ½-inch-wide strip of beaten egg along top edge of pasta. Fold pasta over mousse. Press out all air pockets, then press adjoining edges to seal. Using fluted or plain pastry wheel, separate individual tortelli. Arrange tortelli in single layer on towel-lined baking sheet. Repeat with remaining pasta and mousse. Cover with towel and refrigerate until ready to use.

For vinaigrette: combine vinegar and shallot in blender. With machine running, add oil in very thin steady stream. Season with salt and pepper. Mix in snipped fresh chives.

Bring large amount of salted water to rapid boil. Stir in tortelli. Cook until firm but tender to the bite (al dente), about 5 minutes. Drain well. Pour vinaigrette into large bowl. Add tortelli and toss. Serve immediately.

*Chive Vinegar

Makes 3½ quarts

8 ounces fresh chives
3½ quarts distilled white vinegar
Additional fresh chives (garnish)

Wash chives briefly under running water. Drain in colander 1 to 2 hours.

Add chives to fill ⅔ of 1-gallon container. Fill with vinegar, leaving ¼-inch head space. Cover tightly with plastic wrap or lid. Store mixture in cool place (55°F to 60°F) until flavor develops, 3 to 4 weeks.

Strain vinegar through fine sieve set over large glass or ceramic container. Let vinegar stand overnight.

Insert fresh chives into sterilized jars for garnish and identification. Carefully pour vinegar through funnel into jars, being careful not to disturb any sediment in bottom of container. Cap or seal bottle. Store vinegar in cool dark area until ready to use.

Shrimp and Feta Cheese Sauce à la Grecque

A variation of the sauce served at waterfront tavernas *on the Greek island of Hydra. Feta cheese is salty, so be careful when adding salt to sauce.*

4 servings

12 ounces medium shrimp, cooked, shelled and deveined
1 pound feta cheese, rinsed, patted dry and crumbled
6 green onions, finely chopped
4 teaspoons minced fresh oregano or 1½ teaspoons dried, crumbled
4 tomatoes, peeled, cored, seeded and coarsely chopped
Salt and freshly ground pepper

1 pound pasta, freshly cooked and drained

Combine shrimp, feta, onion, oregano, tomatoes, salt and pepper in large bowl. Let mixture stand at room temperature for at least 1 hour.

Add pasta to sauce and toss to coat well. Serve immediately.

Tricolored Fusilli with Shrimp and Roasted Peppers

4 servings

1 large red bell pepper
1 large green bell pepper

12 ounces mixed egg, spinach and tomato fusilli
Salt and freshly ground pepper

½ cup white wine vinegar
1 tablespoon Dijon mustard
½ cup olive oil
8 ounces small cooked shrimp, shelled and deveined
2 to 3 tablespoons chopped fresh basil leaves

Char peppers in broiler or over open flame, turning until skins blacken. Wrap in plastic bag and steam 10 minutes. Remove skin and seeds. Rinse and pat dry. Cut into fusilli-size strips.

Cook fusilli in large pot of rapidly boiling salted water until firm but still tender to bite. Drain, rinse under cool water and drain again. Sprinkle with salt and pepper. Cool to room temperature.

Blend vinegar, mustard and salt and pepper to taste in bowl. Whisk in oil in thin stream. Add peppers, fusilli, shrimp and basil and toss well. Let stand at room temperature 2 hours before serving.

Shrimp and Feta with Rice Flour Pasta

6 servings

Pasta
1½ cups unbleached all purpose flour
1½ cups rice flour
1 teaspoon salt
4 eggs, beaten
3 tablespoons olive oil

6 cups water
¼ cup vegetable oil
1 tablespoon salt

Shrimp
1 cup dry white wine
½ cup fresh orange juice
2 tablespoons vegetable oil
12 jumbo shrimp, shelled and deveined

Dressing **(makes about 3 cups)**
8 ounces feta cheese, rinsed if salty
3 tablespoons fresh lemon juice
4 garlic cloves, halved
2 cups olive oil
2 tablespoons wine vinegar
1 tablespoon coarsely ground pepper

8 green onions (including green part), trimmed and chopped
2 medium oranges, peeled and sectioned
Red cabbage leaves
Lemon and lime slices (garnish)

For pasta: Sift flours and salt onto work surface. Make well in center. Add eggs to well, mixing with hands. Blend in oil 1 tablespoon at a time. Knead dough until smooth, about 2 to 3 minutes. Let dough rest in refrigerator for 30 minutes.

Feed through pasta machine, gradually narrowing rollers to thinnest setting. Cut into narrowest possible noodles.

Combine water, ¼ cup oil and 1 tablespoon salt in large saucepan and bring to rapid boil over high heat. Add pasta and cook until al dente, about 2 minutes. Drain well. Transfer to bowl. Chill thoroughly.

For shrimp: Bring wine, orange juice and 2 tablespoons oil to boil in large saucepan over high heat. Add shrimp, cover and cook until just opaque, about 5 to 7 minutes. Cover and chill in liquid.

For dressing: Combine cheese, lemon juice and garlic in processor and puree. With machine running, add olive oil, vinegar and pepper and blend thoroughly.

Summer Pastas

Pasta for summer? Yes indeed. Because it teams so well with the vegetables and seafood that are such integral parts of warm-weather dining, and because it can be delicious cold, pasta becomes the perfect base for a variety of meals that are both light and satisfying.

Pasta is, of course, one of the most popular foods around these days, and homemade pasta is in a class unto itself. With the help of a food processor to mix and knead the dough (it takes just 40 seconds) and either a hand-operated or electric pasta machine to roll it out, it's an easy matter to make your own pasta from scratch. Or you can use a rolling pin to roll it out—a little more trouble, but still worth it. Homemade pasta requires brief drying and even briefer cooking—sometimes only a minute or less, depending on your preference, but always less time than store-bought pasta requires. If your time is so limited that even these machine shortcuts do not bring homemade pasta within the realm of possibility, buy the pasta and put your processor to work on the toppings.

Pasta can be made with all purpose unbleached flour, semolina and instant flour, and flavored with your choice of ingredients. You will find that it offers an excellent platform for improvisation.

Pasta's versatility shows itself, too, in the ease with which it can be served as a first course, main dish or salad, hot or at room temperature, for festive occasions as well as everyday meals.

Combine pasta, 2 cups dressing, green onions and orange sections in large bowl and toss gently. Line large salad bowl or individual plates with red cabbage leaves. Drain shrimp. Spoon pasta onto cabbage. Top with shrimp. Garnish with lemon and lime slices. Serve immediately, passing remaining dressing separately.

Pasta with Shrimp and Vegetables

4 servings

¾ cup (1½ sticks) butter
2 small garlic cloves, minced
20 fresh or frozen large shrimp, shelled and deveined
½ small eggplant, halved and thinly sliced
4 large mushrooms, sliced
½ teaspoon dried oregano, crumbled
½ teaspoon dried thyme, crumbled
½ teaspoon dried basil, crumbled
1 medium zucchini, thinly sliced
1 pound spaghetti, freshly cooked and drained
Freshly grated Parmesan cheese

Melt ¼ cup butter in large skillet over medium-high heat. Add garlic and sauté 1 minute. Add shrimp and cook until pink, about 2 minutes on each side. Remove shrimp from skillet using slotted spoon and set aside. Add remaining ½ cup butter to skillet and melt. Add eggplant, mushrooms, oregano, thyme and basil and sauté 2 minutes. Add zucchini and continue cooking until vegetables are tender, about 2 minutes. Reduce heat to low. Return shrimp to skillet and heat through. Arrange vegetables and shrimp over spaghetti. Top with remaining garlic butter from skillet. Sprinkle with Parmesan and serve immediately.

Sauce Niçoise

Small shell pasta is best with Sauce Niçoise, which improves in flavor if prepared a day ahead.

4 servings

24 Greek or black olives, pitted and halved
2 cups fresh green beans, cut into 1½-inch pieces and blanched
½ cup plus 2 tablespoons fresh lemon juice
6 tablespoons olive oil
2 tablespoons Dijon mustard
1 tablespoon minced fresh oregano

1½ to two 10-ounce cans water-packed tuna, well drained and flaked

1 bunch green onions, finely chopped
4 hard-cooked eggs, sliced
Salt and freshly ground pepper

1 pound small shell pasta, freshly cooked and drained
Anchovy fillets (optional garnish)

Combine olives, beans, lemon juice, olive oil, mustard and oregano in large bowl and blend well. Let marinate in refrigerator for several hours.

Add tuna, onion, egg, salt and pepper to marinade and mix gently. Cover and refrigerate for several hours.

When ready to serve, add pasta to sauce and toss well. Garnish with anchovy.

Tuna Mayonnaise

This tasty sauce is especially attractive with spinach pasta.

4 servings

1 10-ounce can water-packed tuna, well drained
½ cup plus 1 tablespoon mayonnaise (preferably homemade)
12 pitted large black olives, sliced
3 tablespoons fresh lemon juice
2 tablespoons capers, rinsed and drained
2 tablespoons minced fresh parsley
Salt and freshly ground pepper

1 pound pasta, freshly cooked and drained

Puree tuna in processor or blender. Transfer to mixing bowl. Add mayonnaise, olives, lemon juice, capers, parsley, salt and pepper and blend well.

Combine pasta and mayonnaise in shallow large serving bowl and toss well. Serve immediately.

5 Pasta with Poultry and Meat

Combine poultry or meat with pasta and you have a robust centerpiece to family and company meals alike. This chapter features all manner of meats as well as chicken in the starring role.

Many of the dishes are well suited to advance preparation. Sauces and fillings can usually be made well ahead of time and reheated, and in most cases the flavor will be all the better for it. "Assembled" dishes such as lasagne and ravioli can, as a rule, be prepared ahead and refrigerated or even frozen before cooking.

On their home ground, most of the Italian specialties in this chapter would be served as a separate pasta course, but all are substantial enough to constitute the meal's main event. Some, like Pappardelle with Rabbit Sauce (page 71), are classics. Others are terrific new twists on familiar dishes—for example, Green Ravioli with Chicken Liver-Walnut Filling (page 70), Red, White and Green Lasagne (page 73) and Pesto Lasagne (page 75). These hearty combinations need little more than a salad and a full-bodied bottle of wine to make a splendid special-occasion dinner.

Spinach Fettuccine with Chicken and Pesto

4 servings

1 cup whipping cream
1 cup (2 sticks) unsalted butter, cut into pieces
3/4 cup freshly grated Parmesan cheese

2 tablespoons olive oil
2 whole chicken breasts, skinned, boned and cut into bite-size pieces

4 tablespoons prepared pesto sauce

12 ounces spinach fettuccine, cooked al dente and drained
Salt and freshly ground pepper
Additional freshly grated Parmesan cheese

Heat cream in heavy small saucepan over medium heat. Add butter and stir until melted. Gradually add 3/4 cup Parmesan and stir until melted. Reduce heat to low; keep sauce warm.

Heat oil in heavy large skillet over medium heat. Add chicken and stir until just opaque, about 3 minutes. Transfer to bowl using slotted spoon. Mix in 1 tablespoon pesto. Toss cooked pasta with remaining 3 tablespoons pesto and cheese sauce. Arrange pasta on platter. Spoon chicken over. Season with salt and pepper. Serve immediately, passing additional Parmesan separately.

Pasta with Chicken "In the Pink" with Four Cheeses

4 servings

5 tablespoons unsalted butter
1 tablespoon olive oil
1 medium onion, chopped
1 garlic clove, minced
3 cups canned whole plum tomatoes in puree
Salt and freshly ground pepper

1 1/2 cups whipping cream

1 pound tubular pasta (such as penne, rigatoni or ziti)
2 large whole chicken breasts, skinned, boned, trimmed, patted dry and shredded

1/2 cup freshly grated pecorino or Parmesan cheese
1/2 cup freshly grated Bel Paese or Fontina cheese
1/3 to 1/2 cup Gorgonzola cheese, crumbled
1/4 cup ricotta cheese
2 tablespoons minced fresh parsley
Additional grated pecorino or Parmesan cheese

Melt 1 tablespoon butter with oil in heavy large saucepan over medium-low heat. Add onion, cover and cook until translucent, stirring occasionally, about 10 minutes. Add garlic and stir 1 minute. Blend in tomatoes. Increase heat to medium-high and simmer uncovered until thickened, stirring occasionally, about 10 minutes. Season lightly with salt and generously with freshly ground pepper.

Bring cream to boil in heavy large skillet. Reduce heat and simmer until slightly thickened, about 5 minutes. Stir in tomato sauce. Keep sauce warm.

Cook pasta in large amount of boiling salted water until al dente (firm to bite). When pasta is almost done, return sauce to simmer. Add chicken to sauce and stir until pieces are just firm, about 2 minutes. Blend in cheeses and remaining 4 tablespoons butter. Drain pasta. Add to sauce, tossing to coat. Adjust seasoning. Spoon mixture into heated bowls. Garnish with minced parsley and serve. Pass additional grated cheese separately.

Golden Chicken with Saffron Pasta

8 servings

- 7 pounds tomatoes, peeled and seeded
- 1/4 cup olive oil
- 4 large leeks (white part only), halved lengthwise and cut into 1/4-inch-thick slices
- 1 1-pound fennel bulb (tough outer stalks discarded and strings removed), cored and cut into 1/4-inch-thick slices, fronds reserved
- 1 large garlic clove, minced
- 2 cups rich chicken stock (preferably homemade)
- 2 cups dry Gewürztraminer
- 2 teaspoons curry powder
- 1/2 teaspoon saffron threads, crushed
- 8 chicken breast halves, skinned and boned
- 1/3 cup crème fraîche
- Salt
- Saffron Pasta (see page 7)
- 1 tablespoon olive oil

Coarsely chop tomatoes in processor in batches, using on/off turns. Divide 1/4 cup oil between 2 heavy large skillets and warm over low heat. Divide leeks, sliced fennel and garlic between skillets. Cover and cook 7 minutes, stirring occasionally. Divide tomatoes, stock, wine and curry powder between skillets and boil until reduced to 3 1/4 cups each, 30 to 45 minutes.

Pour mixtures into 1 skillet. Stir 1/4 cup into saffron; return to skillet and set aside. *(Sauce can be prepared 2 days ahead. Cover and refrigerate.)*

Remove tendon from underside of each chicken breast. Lightly pound breasts between 2 pieces of waxed paper so small fillet on underside adheres and breasts are of uniform thickness. Stir crème fraîche into sauce and bring to boil. Season with salt and adjust other seasonings. Pat chicken dry and push down into sauce. Immediately reduce heat so liquid is barely shaking. Cook chicken 4 minutes. Turn and cook until opaque and just firm to touch, about 3 minutes longer.

Meanwhile, cook pasta in large pot of rapidly boiling salted water until al dente (firm to the bite), 3 to 4 minutes. Drain well. Toss pasta with remaining 1 tablespoon oil and season with salt. Divide among heated plates. Top with chicken and sauce. Garnish with reserved fennel fronds and serve.

Chicken Spaghetti

4 to 6 servings

- 1/4 cup olive oil
- 2 whole chicken breasts, boned, skinned and cut into bite-size pieces
- 8 ounces mushrooms, sliced (about 3 cups)
- 3 tablespoons diced green bell pepper
- 2 tablespoons minced onion
- 2 teaspoons minced garlic
- 1 15-ounce can tomato sauce
- 1/3 cup red wine
- 1 bay leaf
- 2 tablespoons chopped fresh parsley
- 2 teaspoons dried oregano, crumbled
- 1/2 teaspoon freshly ground black pepper
- Dash of hot pepper sauce
- 1 pound spaghetti or capellini, freshly cooked and drained
- 1/4 cup freshly grated Parmesan or Romano cheese

Heat oil in large skillet over medium heat. Sauté chicken pieces until golden brown, about 5 minutes. Remove with slotted spoon and set aside. Add mushrooms, green pepper, onion and garlic to skillet and sauté 2 minutes. Pour off excess oil, if necessary. Reduce heat to low. Add tomato sauce, wine, bay leaf, parsley, oregano, black pepper and hot sauce. Simmer 25 minutes.

Add chicken to skillet and continue simmering 15 more minutes. Discard bay leaf. Arrange spaghetti on platter and pour sauce over. Top with grated cheese. Serve immediately.

Easy Linguine Romano

4 to 6 servings

8 ounces linguine
1/4 cup (1/2 stick) butter
4 ounces chicken livers
3/4 cup (or more) whipping cream
1/2 cup (or more) freshly grated Parmesan cheese
Salt and freshly ground pepper

Cook linguine according to package directions until al dente. Drain well. Meanwhile, melt half the butter in medium skillet over medium-high heat. Add chicken livers and sauté until firm, about 3 minutes; *do not overcook*. Let livers cool, then chop coarsely.

Combine all ingredients in heavy saucepan. Place over low heat and mix gently, adding more cheese or cream to reach desired consistency. Serve immediately.

Green Ravioli with Chicken Liver-Walnut Filling

2 servings

Filling
1 tablespoon walnut or vegetable oil
3 ounces chicken livers
2 tablespoons dry Marsala
Pinch of ground sage
1/2 cup coarsely chopped toasted walnuts
1/4 cup freshly grated Parmesan cheese
1 egg yolk, beaten to blend
Salt and freshly ground pepper
Pinch of freshly grated nutmeg

Sauce
2 tablespoons (1/4 stick) butter
2 tablespoons all purpose flour
1 cup (or more) chicken stock

Pasta
1 cup all purpose flour
2 ounces cooked, drained and squeezed-dry spinach
1 egg
1 tablespoon olive oil
1/2 teaspoon salt
2 tablespoons sour cream, room temperature
2 tablespoons freshly grated Parmesan cheese
1 tablespoon minced fresh parsley
Pinch of freshly grated nutmeg
Additional freshly grated Parmesan cheese (optional)

For filling: Heat walnut oil in heavy medium skillet over medium-high heat. Add livers and sauté until firm, about 3 minutes. Add Marsala and sage and cook until liquid is almost evaporated, about 2 minutes. Cool completely.

Finely chop livers in processor or by hand. Transfer to bowl. Stir in walnuts, 1/4 cup Parmesan and yolk. Season with salt, pepper and nutmeg.

For sauce: Melt butter in heavy medium saucepan over medium-low heat. Add flour and whisk 3 minutes. Whisk in 1 cup stock. Increase heat and bring to boil, whisking constantly. Reduce heat and simmer until thick and smooth, whisking occasionally, about 10 minutes. Set sauce aside.

For pasta: Mound flour on work surface and make well in center. Add spinach, egg, oil and salt to well and blend with fork. Gradually draw flour from inner edge of well into center until all flour is incorporated, adding cold water a few drops at a time if necessary to bind dough. Gather dough into ball. Knead until smooth and shiny, about 10 minutes. (Dough can also be prepared in food processor.)

Cut dough in half. Flatten 1 piece of dough (keep other piece covered to prevent drying) with heel of hand, then fold in half. Turn pasta machine to widest setting and run dough through several times (number will depend on how vigorously dough was kneaded by hand) until smooth and velvety, dusting lightly with flour if sticky. Adjust machine to next narrower setting. Run dough through machine. Repeat, narrowing rollers until pasta is 1/16 inch thick. Cut sheet into two 12 × 4-inch rectangles. Dry sheets until edges begin to curl slightly.

To assemble, set 1 rectangle on work surface. Mark off 2 rows of 2-inch squares. Mound 1 teaspoon filling in center of each square. Cover with second rectangle of pasta, aligning edges. Press down with fingers around each mound of filling. Cut out squares with pastry cutter. Arrange squares on floured kitchen towel. Repeat rolling and assembling with remaining dough.

Bring large amount of salted water to boil. Lower ravioli into water with slotted spoon and cook until firm but just tender to bite (al dente), 7 to 8 minutes, adjusting heat to keep water at gentle boil. Drain on paper towels.

Stir sour cream, 2 tablespoons Parmesan, parsley, nutmeg, salt and pepper into sauce. Bring to simmer and cook 5 minutes (if thinner consistency is desired, add more chicken stock). Divide ravioli between shallow bowls. Pour sauce over and serve, passing additional grated Parmesan if desired.

Pappardelle with Rabbit Sauce Ligurian Style (Pappardelle con Sugo di Coniglio alla Ligure)

4 to 6 servings

Pappardelle

3 cups all purpose flour, preferably unbleached
4 eggs, room temperature

Rabbit Sauce

1 3½- to 4-pound rabbit, cut into 8 to 10 pieces and patted dry
3 tablespoons fresh rosemary, finely ground
3 medium garlic cloves, finely chopped
¼ cup olive oil
1 cup (or more) dry white wine
Salt and freshly ground pepper
5 medium tomatoes, peeled, cored, seeded and finely diced
1 cup pitted green olives
2 tablespoons capers (optional)

1 tablespoon olive or vegetable oil

Butter

For pappardelle: Arrange flour in mound on work surface and make well in center. Break eggs into well and blend with fork. Gradually draw small amount of flour from inner edge of well into eggs with fork, stirring constantly until all flour is incorporated. Gather dough into loose mass and set aside. Scrape any hard bits of flour from work surface and discard. Lightly flour work surface and hands. Knead dough until smooth and elastic, 10 to 12 minutes. Insert finger in center of dough; if dry, dough is ready for pasta machine; if sticky, sprinkle dough lightly with flour and continue kneading until dough is correct consistency.

Cut off 1 egg-size piece of dough. Store remaining dough in plastic wrap or dry towel to prevent drying; set aside. Flatten piece of dough with heel of hand, then fold in half. Turn pasta machine to widest setting and run dough through. Continue folding and kneading process with machine until dough is smooth and velvety, about 2 more times (number will depend on how vigorously dough was kneaded by hand). Dust dough lightly with more flour as necessary.

Adjust pasta machine to next narrower setting. Run dough through machine *without folding*, dusting lightly with flour if sticky. Repeat, narrowing rollers after each run until machine is on second to narrowest setting; pasta should be less than 1/16 inch thick.

Knead and shape remaining dough into sheets, kneading each egg-size piece of dough slightly before running through machine. Set aside until sheets look firm and leathery and edges begin to curl up slightly but are not brittle. This will take 10 to 30 minutes depending on dryness of dough and temperature and humidity of kitchen. *Pasta must be cut at this point or dough will be too brittle.*

To shape pappardelle, cut 1 dough sheet into 1/2-inch-wide strips using fluted pastry wheel. Arrange strips, overlapping as little as possible, on kitchen towel set over baking sheet. Repeat with remaining dough sheets. *(Can be left overnight to dry completely in cool dry place.)*

For sauce: Rub rabbit pieces with rosemary and garlic. Heat 1/4 cup oil in large skillet over medium heat. Add rabbit and cook on all sides until lightly golden, about 10 minutes. Reduce heat to low, pour in 1 cup wine and stir gently to scrape up any browned bits. Season rabbit with salt and pepper. Cover partially and cook 30 minutes, turning meat occasionally and adding more wine if mixture becomes too dry. Add tomatoes and olives. Cover and cook until rabbit is tender, 10 to 20 more minutes. Stir in capers, if desired. Taste sauce and season with salt and pepper. Remove from heat and set aside.

Meanwhile, fill pasta cooker or stockpot 3/4 full with salted water and bring to rapid boil over high heat. Stir in 1 tablespoon oil. Add pappardelle and stir vigorously to prevent sticking. Cook until just firm but tender to bite (al dente), about 5 to 20 seconds for freshly made and up to 3 minutes for thoroughly dried pasta. Taste often to prevent overcooking. Drain.

Butter heated serving platter. Add pasta and toss lightly. Place rabbit mixture over high heat and stir until hot. Add several tablespoons sauce to pasta and blend gently. Arrange rabbit in center of pasta. Serve immediately, passing remaining sauce separately.

Blanquette de Veau with Fresh Pasta

4 servings

1 pound large mushrooms, caps cut into 1/8-inch pieces (stems reserved)
3/4 cup water
1 tablespoon butter
Pinch of salt

2 pounds veal shoulder, trimmed and cut into 1- to 1 1/2-inch pieces
Salt and freshly ground pepper
1 cup dry white wine
2 carrots
2 leeks (with 2 inches of green), quartered and washed
1/2 medium onion
3 to 4 tarragon sprigs
3 thyme sprigs
1 small celery stalk (with leaves), coarsely chopped
1 bay leaf
2 to 3 garlic cloves, unpeeled

1 pound baby carrots (or 4 regular carrots, halved lengthwise and cut into thirds)

1 cup whipping cream
Salt

5 egg yolks
Fresh pasta*

Combine mushroom caps, water, butter and salt in medium saucepan. Cover and bring to boil over high heat. Remove from heat and drain well, reserving liquid. Set aside.

Sprinkle veal generously with salt and pepper. Transfer to 6-quart saucepan or Dutch oven. Add wine and enough water to cover and bring to boil over high heat, skimming any foam that accumulates on surface for the first 5 to 7 minutes. Tie carrots, leek, onion, tarragon, thyme, celery and bay leaf in cheesecloth and add to veal with reserved mushroom stems and unpeeled garlic. Reduce heat, cover and simmer until veal is tender, 50 to 60 minutes.

Meanwhile, blanch baby carrots in boiling water in medium saucepan until tender, about 3 minutes. Drain immediately and plunge into ice water to stop cooking process. Drain again.

Transfer meat to platter. Discard cheesecloth bag from stock. Increase heat to medium and reduce stock by 1/3. Strain stock into bowl, pressing vegetables with back of wooden spoon to extract as much liquid as possible. Return stock to saucepan or Dutch oven. Add reserved mushroom liquid and 1/2 cup cream. Cook over medium heat until reduced by another 1/3. Season with salt to taste. *(Sauce can be prepared ahead to this point, covered and refrigerated up to 2 days. Rewarm slowly over low heat before serving.)*

Beat egg yolks with remaining 1/2 cup cream in medium bowl until well blended. Whisk about 3 tablespoons of warm sauce into yolk mixture, then add mixture to sauce. Cook over medium heat, stirring constantly, until sauce coats spoon; *do not boil.* Return meat, carrot and mushrooms to pan, stirring into sauce. Cook until just heated through. Transfer to platter and serve immediately with freshly cooked pasta.

*Fresh Pasta

4 to 6 servings

3 egg yolks
2 eggs
2 tablespoons whipping cream
1 teaspoon salt
3 cups all purpose flour
Softened butter

Butter
Salt

Whisk egg yolks, eggs, cream and salt in large bowl. Mix in flour until dough leaves sides of bowl. Form into ball. Turn out onto lightly floured surface and knead about 10 minutes. Coat with softened butter to prevent drying. Cover and refrigerate 2 hours.

Roll dough out on lightly floured work surface until paper thin and translucent, stretching and sprinkling with additional flour to prevent sticking. Let dry for 30 minutes.

Roll dough up lengthwise and slice into thin strips. Unroll into rapidly boiling salted water and cook until al dente, about 3 to 4 minutes. Remove from heat and drain well. Rinse in cold water and drain again. Melt butter in large skillet over medium heat. Add pasta and toss until heated through. Season with salt.

Red, White and Green Lasagne (Vincisgrassi)

This lasagne freezes better uncooked.

6 to 8 servings

Pasta

6 13 × 3-inch fresh egg pasta rectangles (about 1 pound), homemade or commercial
3 13 × 3-inch fresh spinach pasta rectangles (about 8 ounces), homemade or commercial

Sauce

¼ cup (½ stick) unsalted butter
¼ cup olive oil
1 large carrot, quartered
1 large onion, quartered
1 pound ground veal
½ cup *each* coarsely chopped chicken hearts and giblets
½ cup dry white wine
1 cup chicken stock
2 tablespoons tomato sauce
1 cup (about) milk
½ cup coarsely chopped chicken livers
6 large mushrooms, coarsely chopped (optional)
Salt and freshly ground pepper

Besciamella

¼ cup (½ stick) butter
⅓ cup all purpose flour
2 cups milk
Freshly grated nutmeg
Salt and freshly ground pepper

6 to 9 tablespoons freshly grated Parmesan cheese
3 tablespoons butter, cut into small pieces
1 tablespoon butter, melted

For pasta: Bring salted water to boil in large saucepan over medium-high heat. Add pasta rectangles one at a time and cook until al dente. Drain; spread out on dampened kitchen towels.

For sauce: Heat ¼ cup butter and ¼ cup oil in large saucepan over medium-high heat. Add carrot and onion and sauté until softened, about 10 minutes. Remove vegetables from oil and discard. Stir in veal, chicken hearts and giblets. Gradually blend in wine. Cook until wine has evaporated. Reduce heat, add stock and tomato sauce and simmer 1 hour, stirring in milk as necessary to keep sauce from becoming too thick. Add chicken livers and mushrooms to sauce and simmer another 30 minutes. Season with salt and pepper to taste.

For besciamella: Melt butter in medium saucepan over medium heat. Blend in flour. Gradually add milk and cook, stirring constantly, until mixture has thickened, about 4 minutes. Season with nutmeg, salt and pepper to taste.

To assemble, preheat oven to 375°F. Generously butter 9 × 13-inch straight-sided dish. Arrange 3 egg pasta rectangles in bottom of dish. Dot with 10 to 12 tablespoons sauce, then dot sauce with about ⅔ cup besciamella. Sprinkle 2 to 3 tablespoons Parmesan cheese over. Dot with 1 tablespoon butter. Repeat above layering with 1 layer of spinach pasta and another layer of egg pasta. Bake until casserole is hot and bubbly, about 30 minutes. Drizzle with 1 tablespoon melted butter and serve.

Quick Spinach Lasagne

4 servings

1 pound sweet Italian sausage

8 lasagne noodles, cooked al dente
8 ounces ricotta cheese
1 pound fresh spinach, stemmed and chopped
8 ounces mozzarella cheese, grated
1 15½-ounce jar thick spaghetti sauce
2 tablespoons freshly grated Parmesan cheese

Crumble sausage into medium skillet. Cook over medium-high heat until well done, 15 to 20 minutes. Drain thoroughly.

Preheat oven to 350°F. Lightly grease 9 × 9-inch baking dish. Arrange 4 noodles in bottom of dish. Spread with half of ricotta. Top with half of spinach, sausage and mozzarella. Pour half of spaghetti sauce over top. Repeat layering. Sprinkle top with Parmesan. Bake until heated through, 30 minutes. Cool 5 minutes and serve.

Ziti Salad with Sausage

8 servings

- **1/3 cup red wine vinegar**
- **1/2 teaspoon salt**
- **1/4 teaspoon freshly ground pepper**
- **1/4 teaspoon dried rosemary, crumbled**
- **1/4 teaspoon dried oregano, crumbled**
- **1/4 teaspoon dried basil, crumbled**
- **1 1/3 cups olive or vegetable oil or combination**
- **1/4 cup freshly grated Parmesan cheese**
- **12 ounces ziti**
- **2 pounds cooked smoked sausage, thinly sliced**
- **1 pound zucchini, thinly sliced**
- **4 medium tomatoes, cut into wedges**
- **1 medium-size green bell pepper, coarsely chopped**
- **1 cup minced fresh parsley**
- **3 ounces pimiento, chopped**
- **Freshly grated Parmesan cheese**

Combine vinegar, salt, pepper and herbs in small bowl. Whisk in oil in slow steady stream until well blended. Mix in 1/4 cup Parmesan. Set dressing aside.

Cook ziti in 4 to 6 quarts boiling salted water until just firm but tender to the bite (al dente), about 7 minutes. Drain and rinse under cold water until cool. Drain again. Combine ziti and remaining ingredients, except Parmesan, in large bowl. Add half of dressing and toss. Add as much of remaining dressing as necessary to coat salad thoroughly. Sprinkle with additional grated Parmesan, if desired, and serve.

Pesto Lasagne

8 servings

- **12 ounces spicy Italian sausage, casings removed**
- **12 ounces ground beef**
- **12 ounces mushrooms, sliced**
- **1 medium onion, chopped**
- **1/2 cup chopped red or green bell pepper**
- **2 large garlic cloves, minced**
- **1 28-ounce can whole tomatoes, drained**
- **1 6-ounce can tomato paste**
- **1/2 cup sliced black olives**
- **1 small bay leaf**
- **2 1/2 cups Pesto***
- **1 15-ounce container ricotta cheese**
- **8 ounces lasagne noodles, freshly cooked and drained**
- **1 pound mozzarella cheese, shredded**
- **1/3 cup freshly grated Parmesan cheese**

Combine sausage, ground beef, mushrooms, onion, bell pepper and garlic in heavy large saucepan over medium heat. Sauté until onion is translucent, crumbling sausage and beef with fork, about 15 minutes. Drain off liquid. Add tomatoes, tomato paste, olives and bay leaf. Reduce heat to low, cover and simmer 1 1/2 hours, stirring occasionally. Discard bay leaf.

Preheat oven to 350°F. Mix pesto and ricotta in medium bowl. Spoon thin layer of sausage mixture into bottom of 9 × 13-inch baking dish. Top with layer of noodles. Spread some of pesto mixture evenly over top. Sprinkle with some of mozzarella and Parmesan. Repeat layering. Cover with foil. *(Lasagne can be prepared ahead to this point and frozen.)* Bake until top is golden brown, about 40 minutes. Serve hot.

*Pesto

Makes 2½ cups

1½ cups packed fresh basil leaves
⅓ cup olive oil
⅓ cup pine nuts
⅓ cup freshly grated Parmesan cheese
3 large garlic cloves

Combine all ingredients in processor or blender and puree until smooth.

Stuffed Rotolo (Rotolo di Pasta Ripieno)

This dish features a single large sheet of hand-rolled pasta wrapped around a delectable spinach filling. It can be assembled ahead, refrigerated and then baked just before serving.

6 to 8 servings

1 ounce dried Italian mushrooms (porcini)

2½ pounds fresh spinach, stemmed and thoroughly rinsed (about 2½ large bunches), or two 10-ounce packages frozen spinach
1 cup water
1 tablespoon salt
3 tablespoons butter
Salt and freshly ground pepper
⅓ cup freshly grated Parmesan cheese
¼ cup whipping cream

Meat Sauce
3 tablespoons butter
2 sweet Italian sausages (5 to 6 ounces total)
5 to 6 ounces ground veal
½ cup water
1 heaping tablespoon tomato paste
¼ cup whipping cream

Balsamella
¼ cup (½ stick) butter
3 tablespoons all purpose flour
2 cups milk
Salt
Pinch of freshly grated nutmeg

Pasta
1½ cups all purpose flour, preferably unbleached
2 eggs, room temperature

1 tablespoon olive or vegetable oil

Freshly grated Parmesan cheese (about 4 to 6 tablespoons)

Butter

Whipping cream, if necessary (up to ⅓ cup)

Combine dried mushrooms in small bowl with just enough lukewarm water to cover. Let stand until softened, about 30 minutes. Drain mushrooms well and squeeze dry, reserving liquid. Strain liquid through several layers of dampened cheesecloth. Set liquid aside. Discard hard stems; dice caps.

Combine fresh spinach, 1 cup water and 1 tablespoon salt in large pot or Dutch oven over high heat. Cover and simmer until spinach is tender, about 2 to 3 minutes. (If using frozen spinach, cook according to package directions.) Drain spinach and squeeze dry. Melt 3 tablespoons butter in medium skillet over medium-high heat. Mix in spinach. Season with salt and pepper to taste. Blend in ⅓ cup Parmesan with ¼ cup cream and sauté about 2 to 3 minutes. Transfer mixture to processor and chop coarsely using on/off turns; *do not puree.*

For meat sauce: Melt 3 tablespoons butter in medium skillet over medium-high heat. Discard casings from sausage and crumble meat into skillet. Stir in veal and cook, mashing with fork until meat is no longer pink. Add mushrooms and reserved liquid and cook, stirring occasionally, until liquid evaporates, about

5 to 10 minutes. Combine 1/2 cup water with tomato paste and stir into meat mixture. Blend in 1/4 cup cream. Taste and season with salt and pepper. Reduce heat to medium and continue cooking until thick, about 5 to 10 minutes.

For balsamella: Melt 1/4 cup butter in heavy saucepan over low heat. Stir in flour. Let mixture bubble gently 3 minutes, stirring constantly; *do not let flour brown.* Whisk in milk, increase heat to medium-high and continue stirring until sauce boils. Season with salt and nutmeg to taste. Simmer sauce 5 minutes, whisking occasionally. Stir 1/2 cup balsamella into meat sauce. Cover remaining balsamella with piece of lightly greased waxed paper.

For pasta: Arrange flour in mound on work surface and make well in center. Break eggs into well and blend with fork. Gradually draw small amount of flour from inner edge of well into eggs with fork, stirring constantly until all flour is incorporated. Gather dough into loose mass and set aside. Scrape any hard bits of flour from work surface and discard. Lightly flour work surface and hands. Knead dough until smooth and elastic, 10 to 12 minutes. Insert finger in center of dough; if dry, dough is ready for pasta machine; if sticky, sprinkle dough lightly with flour and continue kneading until dough is correct consistency.

Roll dough out evenly with rolling pin on lightly floured surface into 17- to 18-inch circle (about 1/16 inch thick), being sure to roll over edges. Set aside until circle looks firm and leathery and edges begin to curl up slightly but are not brittle. This will take 10 to 30 minutes depending on dryness of dough and temperature and humidity of kitchen.

To cook pasta, fill pasta cooker or stockpot fitted with colander 3/4 full of salted water and bring to rapid boil over high heat. Stir in 1 tablespoon oil. Carefully lower dough sheet into colander (do not let dough bunch up) and cook until just firm but tender to bite (al dente), about 30 to 40 seconds. Remove colander and immediately plunge pasta into cold water to prevent sticking. Drain pasta well.

Preheat oven to 400°F. Generously butter baking dish. Moisten large kitchen towel with cold water. Lay pasta flat on towel. Pat top of pasta dry with paper towel. Using fluted pastry wheel or sharp knife, cut pasta to fit length of baking dish. Spread meat sauce over pasta, leaving 4-inch border on 1 short side and about 1-inch borders on remaining 3 sides. Spread spinach over meat sauce. Sprinkle with 2 to 3 tablespoons Parmesan.

Fold 4-inch border over filling, then roll pasta up lengthwise jelly roll style. Carefully transfer to prepared baking dish. Spread thin layer of balsamella over top, reserving about 1 cup. Sprinkle with 2 to 3 tablespoons Parmesan. Dot with butter. *(Can be prepared ahead to this point. Cover lightly with waxed paper and refrigerate until ready to bake.)*

Bake until cheese is melted and top of roll is golden, about 10 to 15 minutes, pouring up to 1/3 cup cream over top or into dish if mixture seems too dry. Let cool 10 minutes before slicing. Arrange slices on individual plates. Top each with 1 to 2 tablespoons of reserved balsamella. Serve immediately.

Garganelli with Mushrooms, Sausage and Cream Sauce (Garganelli del Ghiottone)

This macaroni is traditionally shaped using a thick ridged plate known as il pettine, *but a large comb with long teeth will also work quite well.*

4 servings

Garganelli

- **2 cups all purpose flour (preferably unbleached)**
- **3 eggs, room temperature**

Mushroom, Sausage and Cream Sauce

- **1 ounce dried Italian mushrooms (porcini)**
- **1/4 cup (1/2 stick) butter**
- **2 sweet Italian sausages (5 to 6 ounces total)**
- **3/4 cup dry white wine**
- **1 1/4 cups whipping cream**
- **1 tablespoon minced fresh parsley**
- **1/8 teaspoon ground saffron, dissolved in 2 tablespoons hot water**
- **Freshly ground pepper**
- **Salt (optional)**
- **1 tablespoon olive or vegetable oil**
- **3/4 cup (or more) freshly grated Parmesan cheese**

For garganelli: Arrange flour in mound on work surface and make well in center. Break eggs into well and blend with fork. Gradually draw small amount of flour from inner edge of well into eggs with fork, stirring constantly until all flour is incorporated. Gather dough into loose mass and set aside. Scrape any hard bits of flour from work surface and discard. Lightly flour work surface and hands. Knead dough until smooth and elastic, 10 to 12 minutes. Insert finger in center of dough; if dry, dough is ready for pasta machine; if sticky, sprinkle dough lightly with flour and continue kneading until dough is correct consistency.

Cut off 1 egg-size piece of dough. Store remaining dough in plastic wrap or dry towel to prevent drying; set aside. Flatten piece of dough with heel of hand, then fold in half. Turn pasta machine to widest setting and run dough through. Continue folding and kneading process with pasta machine until dough is smooth and velvety, about 2 more times (number will depend on how vigorously dough was kneaded by hand). Dust dough lightly with more flour as necessary.

Adjust pasta machine to next narrower setting. Run dough through machine *without folding,* dusting lightly with flour if sticky. Repeat, narrowing rollers after each run until machine is on second to narrowest setting; pasta should be less than 1/16 inch thick.

The first dough sheet must be cut and shaped before forming remaining sheets or dough will be too brittle. Knead each piece of dough slightly before running through machine. To shape garganelli, immediately cut dough sheet into 1 1/2-inch squares using fluted pastry wheel or sharp knife. Arrange large comb with long teeth on work surface, teeth pointing away from you. Lay 1 pasta square diagonally across center of comb. Position chopstick or pencil parallel to comb on tip of corner that is pointing toward you. Curl corner around chopstick, then roll chopstick forward, pressing down lightly until entire square is rolled up to form ridged pasta tube, pointed on each end. Carefully slide garganelli off chopstick onto kitchen towel set over baking sheet. Repeat with remaining dough. Let garganelli dry at room temperature until ready to cook.

For sauce: Combine mushrooms in small bowl with just enough lukewarm water to cover. Let stand until softened, about 30 minutes. Drain mushrooms well and squeeze dry, reserving liquid. Strain liquid through several layers of cheesecloth; set aside. Discard hard stems; dice mushroom caps.

Melt butter in large skillet over medium heat. Discard casings from sausage. Crumble meat into skillet and cook, mashing with fork to break up lumps, until meat is no longer pink. Increase heat to medium-high, pour in wine and cook until wine evaporates, about 10 minutes, stirring occasionally. Stir in mushrooms and reserved liquid and continue cooking until almost all liquid is evaporated.

Add cream, parsley, saffron and pepper. Bring mixture to simmer and cook until liquid is reduced to saucelike consistency, stirring occasionally. Taste and season with salt. Keep warm.

Meanwhile, fill pasta cooker or stockpot 3/4 full with salted water and bring to rapid boil over high heat. Stir in oil. Add garganelli and stir vigorously to prevent sticking. Cook until just firm but tender to bite (al dente), about 5 to 20 seconds for freshly made and up to 3 minutes for thoroughly dried pasta. Taste often to prevent overcooking. Drain.

Add pasta to sauce. Sprinkle with 3/4 cup Parmesan. Place over low heat and mix gently until sauce is heated through and pasta is well coated. Transfer to heated platter and serve immediately. Pass additional Parmesan, if desired.

Shells à la Thom

8 to 10 servings

Savory Italian Tomato Sauce*
1 tablespoon butter
1 15- to 16-ounce container ricotta cheese
1 pound medium or large macaroni shells, freshly cooked and drained
1/3 cup chopped Italian parsley
2 tablespoons freshly grated Parmesan or Romano cheese
Salt and freshly ground pepper

Prepare sauce and keep warm.

Melt butter in large skillet over low heat. Add ricotta and stir until melted. Add pasta, turning until well coated. Sprinkle parsley and Parmesan or Romano cheese over top and toss gently. Season with salt and pepper. Transfer to platter. Ladle some of sauce over top and serve immediately, passing remaining tomato sauce at table.

*Savory Italian Tomato Sauce

Makes about 2 1/2 quarts

3 tablespoons olive oil
1 pound sweet Italian sausage, cut into 1-inch pieces
3 large garlic cloves, minced
3/4 cup chopped onion
2 6-ounce cans tomato paste
2 28-ounce cans whole peeled tomatoes, drained and chopped
1/2 cup water
1/4 cup chopped fresh parsley
2 bay leaves
1 1/2 tablespoons chopped fresh basil or 1 teaspoon dried, crumbled
1 teaspoon dried oregano, crumbled
1/2 teaspoon freshly ground pepper
1/8 teaspoon sugar

Heat oil in 4-quart saucepan over medium-high heat. Add sausage and sauté until no longer pink, about 10 minutes. Add garlic and onion and sauté until onion is translucent and sausage is browned and crumbly, about 10 minutes. Blend in tomato paste. Cook 5 minutes. Add remaining ingredients. Reduce heat, cover and simmer about 35 to 45 minutes. Taste and adjust seasoning.

Fettuccine Verdi Capriccio

8 first-course servings

- 4 ounces lean slab bacon, cut into small cubes
- 10 black olives, halved and pitted
- 2 cups tomato sauce (preferably homemade)
- 1/4 cup (1/2 stick) unsalted butter
- 2 cups whipping cream
- 2 tablespoons chopped fresh parsley
- Salt and freshly ground pepper

- 1 1/4 pounds green fettuccine
- 1 cup freshly grated Parmesan cheese

Combine bacon and olives in large skillet over medium heat and cook 5 minutes (do not fry bacon crisp). Drain off all fat. Add tomato sauce and butter to skillet and simmer 2 minutes. Stir in cream, parsley, salt and pepper and cook 2 more minutes. Remove from heat and set aside.

Bring large pot of salted water to rapid boil. Add fettuccine and cook al dente; drain well. Transfer to large bowl. Reheat sauce briefly. Add to pasta and toss gently. Add Parmesan and toss again. Serve hot.

Rigatoni del Curato

Rigatoni "in the mode of a rustic priest"—who must have eaten well.

6 servings

- 2 ounces dried porcini mushrooms
- 3 cups cold water
- 1 1/2 cups hot water

- 3 tablespoons butter
- 5 ounces sliced smoked bacon, blanched 3 minutes and minced (about 8 medium-thick slices)
- 1 large onion, minced
- 1 2-inch fresh rosemary sprig or pinch of dried, crumbled
- 5 fresh basil leaves or 1/4 teaspoon dried, crumbled
- 1 pound fresh mushrooms, sliced
- 2/3 cup dry white wine
- 1 bay leaf
- 1 1/4 cups deglazed and reduced meat juices or 1 quart unsalted poultry or meat stock reduced to 1 1/4 cups

- 1 pound rigatoni
- 2 tablespoons (1/4 stick) unsalted butter

- 2/3 cup half and half or 1/3 cup whipping cream mixed with 1/3 cup milk
- Salt and freshly ground pepper
- 2 cups (about) freshly grated Parmigiano-Reggiano cheese

Combine mushrooms and cold water and stir through once. Let sediment settle, then remove mushrooms with slotted spoon. Discard water. Combine mushrooms and hot water and set aside until soft, 20 to 30 minutes. Remove mushrooms (reserving liquid) and gently squeeze dry. Mince mushrooms, discarding hard core.

Melt butter in heavy large nonaluminum skillet over medium heat. Add bacon and onion with fresh rosemary and fresh basil (if using). Cook just until onion begins to color, about 5 minutes. Push mixture to side, tip skillet and spoon off all but about 4 tablespoons fat. Discard fresh rosemary and fresh basil. Increase heat to medium-high. Add fresh and dried mushrooms and sauté until fresh mushrooms begin to wilt, about 5 minutes. Add wine and bay leaf with dried rosemary and dried basil (if using) and boil until completely evaporated, about 7 minutes. Stir in 1 cup meat juices or reduced stock with reserved mushroom liquid and simmer slowly until liquid is reduced to thick glaze, stirring occasionally. Discard bay leaf. *(Mixture can be prepared up to 2 days ahead to this point and refrigerated.)*

About 1 hour before serving, bring large amount of salted water to rapid boil in large pot. Stir in pasta and cook until just firm and almost tender to the bite (al dente). Drain well. Heat butter in large skillet over medium-high heat. Add mushroom mixture and cook until bubbling. Stir in remaining ¼ cup meat juices or reduced stock and boil until thick.

When ready to serve, bring to boil. Stir in half and half and boil 1 minute. Add pasta and toss gently until mixture is heated through and pasta is well coated, about 3 minutes. Season with salt and pepper to taste. Spoon into large soup bowls. Serve immediately, passing cheese separately.

Pasta can be cooked up to 1 day ahead (though a great violation of Italian tradition, it works). Drain in colander and rinse with warm water; redrain well. Transfer to bowl and toss with 2 tablespoons vegetable oil or butter. Cover and refrigerate. Bring to room temperature before using.

Spaghetti Carbonara with Prosciutto

6 servings

- **5 egg yolks**
- **2 tablespoons olive oil**
- **½ teaspoon minced garlic**
- **8 thin slices prosciutto, chopped**
- **1 pound spaghetti, freshly cooked and drained**
- **⅓ cup half and half**
- **½ cup freshly grated Parmesan cheese**
- **Freshly ground pepper**

Beat yolks in large bowl. Heat oil in medium skillet over medium-high heat. Add garlic and sauté until lightly browned. Add prosciutto and sauté 1 minute. Pour off remaining oil. Add prosciutto mixture and spaghetti to yolks and toss thoroughly. Add half and half and cheese and toss again. Serve immediately, passing pepper separately.

Pasta Riviera

A very flexible recipe that can be adjusted for the amount of ham you have on hand. Orange, tomato and herbs give the sauce its distinctive flavor.

8 servings (about 3⅔ cups sauce)

- **3 pounds fresh tomatoes (preferably plum), peeled and seeded**
- **1 large orange**
- **2 tablespoons olive oil**
- **1 cup chopped onion**
- **1 large garlic clove, minced**
- **¼ teaspoon dried red pepper flakes**
- **½ cup dry white wine**
- **4½ teaspoons chopped fresh oregano or marjoram**
- **1½ teaspoons tomato paste**
- **½ teaspoon sugar**
- **3 tablespoons chopped fresh parsley**
- **2 pounds spaghetti or linguine**
- **2 cups (about) cooked ham, cut into ¼ × ¼ × 1-inch strips**
- **½ cup Niçoise olives**
- **¾ teaspoon coarse salt**
- **2 tablespoons (¼ stick) unsalted butter**

Finely chop tomatoes in batches in processor using on/off turns; do not puree. Set aside for sauce.

Remove peel from orange using vegetable peeler. Reserve two 2-inch strips. Cut remaining peel into very thin julienne. Bring large amount of water to rapid boil. Drop all peel into water and blanch 3 minutes. Drain and rinse well under cold water; drain again. Squeeze juice from orange.

Heat oil in Dutch oven over medium-high heat. Add onion, garlic and red pepper flakes and sauté until beginning to soften, about 3 minutes. Mix in wine, 1½ teaspoons oregano, tomato paste and sugar with reserved tomatoes, orange peel julienne and orange juice. Bring sauce to boil. Reduce heat and simmer until mixture is thickened and little or no watery liquid remains on surface when stirred, about 45 minutes (sauce should measure about 3⅔ cups). Chop reserved orange peel strips. Mix peel with 2 tablespoons parsley; reserve for garnish.

Bring large amount of water to boil in stockpot or pasta cooker. Add pasta and cook until al dente.

Stir ham and olives into sauce. Blend in salt with remaining oregano and parsley. Whisk in butter.

Drain pasta well. Return to stockpot. Add sauce and toss thoroughly. Divide among plates or shallow bowls. Sprinkle with reserved orange peel mixture and serve immediately.

Ravioli of Mushrooms with Pine Nuts, Cured Ham and Cream

6 servings

Mushroom Filling

- 2 tablespoons (¼ stick) unsalted butter
- 2 tablespoons chopped onion
- ½ teaspoon minced garlic
- 12 ounces mixed fresh mushrooms (preferably shiitake, oyster or chanterelle), thinly sliced
- 2 tablespoons brandy
- 1 8-ounce package cream cheese, room temperature
- 1 teaspoon chopped fresh basil or ½ teaspoon dried, crumbled
- 1 teaspoon chopped fresh thyme or ½ teaspoon dried, crumbled
- ½ teaspoon coarse salt
- Pinch of freshly ground white pepper

Pasta

- 4 cups bread flour
- 5 eggs
- 2 tablespoons olive oil
- 1 egg beaten with 1 tablespoon water (glaze)

Sauce

- ½ cup rich chicken stock (preferably homemade)
- 2 tablespoons (¼ stick) unsalted butter
- 8 ounces mixed fresh mushrooms (preferably shiitake, oyster or chanterelle), thinly sliced
- 2 cups whipping cream
- 1 cup freshly grated Parmesan cheese
- ½ cup pine nuts
- 4 ounces cured ham (such as prosciutto or Bayonne), cubed

For filling: Melt butter in heavy medium skillet over medium heat. Add onion and garlic and stir 1 minute. Add mushrooms and stir 3 minutes. Tilt pan, pour brandy into corner, heat and ignite. Continue cooking until all liquid has evaporated, stirring occasionally, about 10 minutes. Cool to room temperature. Transfer to processor and coarsely chop using on/off turns. Add cream cheese, herbs, salt and pepper and mix until well blended; do not puree. Cover and refrigerate until ready to use.

For pasta: Mound flour on work surface and make well in center. Add eggs and olive oil to well and blend with fork. Gradually draw flour from inner edge of well into center until all flour is incorporated. Gather dough into ball. Knead on lightly floured surface until smooth and shiny, about 10 minutes. Wrap in plastic. Let stand at room temperature 15 minutes.

Lightly flour baking sheets. Cut dough into 8 pieces. Flatten 1 piece of dough (keep remainder covered), then fold into thirds. Turn pasta machine to widest setting and run dough through. Repeat until dough is smooth and velvety, folding before each run and dusting with flour if necessary. Adjust pasta machine to next narrower setting. Run dough through without folding. Repeat, narrowing rollers after each run, until pasta is about 1/16 inch thick, dusting with flour occasionally. Lay dough sheet on lightly floured surface. Mound 1 teaspoon filling at 1½-inch intervals along top half of sheet, leaving 1-inch border along edges. Brush dough between filling with glaze. Fold lower half of sheet over filling. Press with fingers around filling to seal and eliminate air pockets. Trim around filling with pastry cutter to create ravioli. Arrange on prepared sheet. Cover with plastic wrap and refrigerate until ready to use. Repeat rolling and assembling with remaining 7 pieces of dough and remaining filling.

For sauce: Boil stock in heavy small saucepan until reduced by half. Melt butter in heavy large skillet over medium heat. Add mushrooms and stir 3 minutes. Add reduced stock, cream, ¼ cup Parmesan cheese and ¼ cup pine nuts. Increase heat to high and boil until sauce coats back of spoon, 15 to 20 minutes.

Bring large pot of salted water to boil. Add ravioli and cook until just tender but firm to bite (al dente). Drain well. Add ravioli and ham to sauce and heat through. Spoon onto platter. Sprinkle with remaining Parmesan and pine nuts and serve immediately.

Tagliolini Verdi Gratinati

6 servings

3½ to 4½ cups all purpose flour
8 ounces spinach, cooked, drained, squeezed dry and finely chopped
4 eggs
1 teaspoon salt
Water

4 to 8 ounces ham, thinly sliced and cut into strips
½ cup freshly grated Parmesan cheese
¼ cup (½ stick) butter, cut into small pieces
½ to ¾ cup béchamel sauce*

Mound 3½ cups flour on work surface. Make a well in center and add spinach, eggs, salt and a few drops of water. Mix with hands, incorporating flour gradually, until dough forms ball, adding more water as necessary to make dough moist but not wet. Divide into several workable pieces.

Working by hand or machine, roll and stretch dough into thin sheet. If working by hand, roll up dough jelly roll fashion. Cut into ¼-inch widths. Carefully unroll pasta onto cloth or board and allow to dry completely. If using machine, allow dough to dry partially, about 1 hour. Set machine on narrow setting and cut dough. Separate pasta and allow to dry completely.

Cook dried pasta in 6 to 8 quarts boiling salted water until al dente, about 4 minutes. Drain well. Turn into ovenproof serving dish. Add ham and all but 2 tablespoons Parmesan. Dot with butter and toss lightly. Cover with béchamel, then sprinkle with remaining Parmesan. Preheat broiler. Place dish about 6 inches from heat until top is light brown, about 3 minutes. Serve immediately.

*For béchamel sauce, use your favorite recipe or prepare balsamella (see recipe for Stuffed Rotolo, page 76), using 4 teaspoons butter, 1 tablespoon all purpose flour, ⅔ cup milk and salt and freshly grated nutmeg to taste.

Homemade Spaghetti Sauce

Made entirely in the microwave.

Makes about 4 cups

- 1 large onion, sliced
- 1/4 cup sliced celery
- 8 medium mushrooms, sliced
- 1/2 green bell pepper, seeded and thinly sliced
- 3 garlic cloves, minced
- 2 tablespoons olive or vegetable oil
- 8 ounces lean ground beef
- 1 14-ounce can whole peeled tomatoes, chopped (reserve juice)
- 1 6-ounce can tomato paste
- 2 tablespoons chopped fresh parsley
- 1 teaspoon minced fresh basil or 1/2 teaspoon dried, crumbled

Combine onion, celery, mushrooms, green pepper, garlic and oil in 2-quart baking dish. Cover and cook in microwave on High for 5 minutes, stirring once. Add ground beef and continue cooking 3 minutes. Stir through several times. Blend in tomatoes with juice, tomato paste, parsley and basil. Cover and cook on High until sauce is slightly thickened, stirring once, about 12 minutes. Serve hot.

Pasta-Beef Salad with Snow Peas and Cauliflower

6 servings

- 4 ounces snow peas, strings removed
- 1 small cauliflower (1 pound), broken into small florets

- 2/3 cup fresh parsley leaves
- 1 large garlic clove
- 2/3 cup vegetable oil
- 1/4 cup red wine vinegar
- 1/4 cup fresh basil, cut into strips, or 1 tablespoon dried, crumbled
- 1 1/2 tablespoons Dijon mustard
- 2 teaspoons sugar
- 2 teaspoons salt
- Freshly ground pepper

- 1 large red bell pepper (6 ounces), cut into 4 rectangular pieces
- 2 large carrots (8 ounces total), peeled and cut into processor feed tube lengths

- 2 medium zucchini (1 pound total), cut into processor feed tube lengths
- 1 medium-size red onion, halved
- 8 ounces freshly cooked semolina fettuccine (see Basic Semolina Pasta, page 2)
- 1 1/4 pounds cooked beef,* cut into 2-inch strips

Cook snow peas in large pot of boiling salted water until crisp-tender. Remove with slotted spoon and drain well. Transfer to 2-quart bowl. Add cauliflower to water. Boil until crisp-tender. Drain well. Add to snow peas.

Using food processor fitted with steel knife, mince parsley. Set aside. With machine running, drop garlic through feed tube and mince. Add oil, vinegar, basil, mustard, sugar, salt and pepper and blend 2 seconds.

Carefully remove steel knife and insert thick slicer. Stand red pepper in feed tube, packing tightly. Slice using light pressure.

Remove thick slicer and insert julienne disc or shredder. Stack carrots horizontally in feed tube and shred using firm pressure.

Remove julienne disc and insert French-fry disc. Stand zucchini in feed tube and cut using medium pressure. Place onion in feed tube and cut using medium pressure. Add mixture to snow peas and cauliflower. Blend in pasta, meat and parsley. *(Can be prepared up to 1 day ahead and refrigerated.)* Taste and adjust seasoning before serving.

*Cooked chicken, seafood, ham or pork can be substituted for the beef.

Meatball-Stuffed Lasagne (Sagne Chine)

A spectacular party entrée, layered with pasta, mushroom-tomato sauce, tiny meatballs, peas, artichoke hearts and cheese. The entire dish can be assembled the day before serving.

6 to 8 servings

Mushroom-Tomato Sauce
- 1 ounce dried porcini mushrooms
- 2 cups warm water

- 2 tablespoons olive oil
- 1/2 cup minced onion
- 1/2 cup minced carrot
- 1/2 cup minced celery
- 1 28-ounce can Italian plum tomatoes, drained (liquid reserved) and coarsely chopped
- Salt and freshly ground pepper

Meatballs
- 8 ounces ground pork
- 1 egg, beaten to blend
- 3 tablespoons freshly grated pecorino cheese
- All purpose flour
- 3 tablespoons olive oil
- 3/4 cup beef stock

Vegetables
- 2 tablespoons olive oil
- 1/4 cup minced onion
- 2 pounds fresh peas, shelled, or one 10-ounce package frozen peas, thawed
- 1 9-ounce package frozen artichoke hearts, thawed and thinly sliced

- 12 ounces shredded mozzarella or provola cheese
- 1 tablespoon olive oil

- Olive oil
- Freshly cooked Semolina Lasagne*
- 3 hard-cooked eggs, coarsely chopped

- 1 1/2 cups freshly grated pecorino cheese
- 1 hard-cooked egg, sliced (optional)

For sauce: Soak mushrooms in warm water until soft, about 30 minutes.

Heat oil in heavy medium saucepan over medium-low heat. Add onion, carrot and celery and cook until soft, stirring occasionally, about 10 minutes. Add tomatoes, salt and pepper. Simmer 30 minutes, stirring frequently and adding reserved tomato liquid if mixture begins to stick. Puree through food mill. Return mixture to pan.

Strain mushrooms through sieve lined with dampened paper towel; reserve liquid. Rinse mushrooms, discard tough center and chop finely. Add to tomatoes with 1 cup soaking liquid. Simmer sauce 20 minutes, stirring frequently and adding more mushroom soaking liquid or tomato liquid if sauce sticks (sauce should be thick enough to hold its shape on spoon). Cool. *(Can be prepared 1 day ahead and refrigerated.)*

For meatballs: Combine pork, egg, cheese, salt and pepper in medium bowl. Form into 3/4-inch meatballs. Dust with flour. Heat oil in heavy large skillet over medium heat. Add meatballs and cook until browned on all sides, about 6 minutes. Remove with slotted spoon. Discard all but 2 tablespoons oil in skillet. Add stock and boil 30 seconds, scraping up any browned bits. Strain stock and set aside. *(Can be prepared 1 day ahead. Refrigerate meatballs and stock separately.)*

For vegetables: Heat 2 tablespoons oil in heavy medium skillet over medium-low heat. Add onion and cook until golden brown, stirring frequently, about 15 minutes. Add fresh peas, artichokes, salt and pepper and cook until vegetables are tender, stirring frequently, about 5 minutes. (If using frozen thawed peas, mix in at this point). Cool to room temperature.

Combine mozzarella, 1 tablespoon oil, salt and pepper in small bowl.

To assemble, generously coat 9 × 13-inch baking dish with olive oil. Arrange pasta strips around edge of pan, overlapping slightly and allowing 4-inch overhang. Cover bottom with pasta, overlapping slightly. Spread 1/3 of sauce over pasta in bottom of dish. Layer with 1/3 of vegetable mixture, 1/3 of chopped eggs,

1/3 of meatballs and 1/3 of mozzarella. Repeat layering twice. Fold in pasta overhang. Cover center of lasagne with additional pasta if necessary. *(Can be prepared 1 day ahead to this point. Brush with olive oil, cover and refrigerate. Bring to room temperature before continuing.)*

Preheat oven to 350°F. Sprinkle top of lasagne with pecorino cheese and ladle reserved meat broth over. Bake until hot in center, about 40 minutes. Cool 10 minutes. Garnish top with egg.

*Semolina Lasagne

Makes about 8 ounces

1 1/2 cups (or more) semolina flour
1/2 teaspoon salt
1/2 cup (scant) lukewarm water (95°F)
All purpose flour
4 tablespoons olive oil

Combine 1 1/2 cups semolina and salt and arrange in mound on work surface. Make well in center and add water. Using fork, gradually incorporate semolina from inner edge of well into center until all semolina is incorporated. Knead until smooth and elastic, adding more semolina if dough is sticky, about 8 minutes. (Can also be prepared in processor. Mix about 45 seconds.) Cover with inverted bowl and let stand 30 minutes.

Cut dough into 6 pieces. Flatten 1 piece of dough (keep remainder covered), then fold into thirds. Turn pasta machine to widest setting and run dough through until smooth and velvety, dusting with flour if sticky and folding before each run, about 10 times. Adjust machine to next narrower setting. Run dough through machine without folding. Repeat narrowing rollers after each run until pasta is 1/16 inch thick. Cut into 8-inch lengths and arrange in single layer on towel. Repeat with remaining dough.

Fill large bowl 3/4 full with cold water; add 2 tablespoons oil. Bring large amount of salted water to rapid boil in large pot; add 2 tablespoons oil. Boil 3 pieces of pasta 30 seconds. Transfer to bowl of cold water, using slotted spoon. Arrange in single layer on wet towel. Cover with another wet towel. Repeat with remaining pasta.

6 Oriental Noodles

Oriental noodles sometimes get overshadowed by all the colors and shapes of their European-style rivals. There is no reason for this to happen, though, because Far Eastern noodles have unique charms of their own.

The oriental types are divided into two classes, wheat-based and starch-based. Those made from wheat (such as Chinese egg noodles and Japanese *udon*) are similar to Western spaghetti or linguine, which can be used in their place. Starch noodles—for example, rice sticks and bean threads—are a very different product. They are translucent and precooked, so they need only be soaked or very briefly cooked before serving.

Whichever type of noodle they employ, oriental dishes provide a refreshing change of pace to those more accustomed to Western-style pasta. Sauces are by turns pungent and mellow, often perfumed with soy sauce, ginger, vinegar and sesame oil. Even the simplest dishes offer sophisticated and subtle flavor combinations. More elaborate dishes such as Thai Fried Noodles (page 94), Cantonese Seafood Noodle (page 95) and Fried Rice Noodles with Barbecued Pork (page 93) boast a spectrum of colors, flavors and textures—sweet and savory, crisp and tender—that are of global appeal.

Fukien Sesame Seed Sauce

A delicate topping for oriental noodles as well as for dim sum, shellfish, chicken or duck.

Makes 1 cup

½ cup lightly toasted sesame seed
⅓ cup thinly sliced green onion, white part only
2 tablespoons light soy sauce
2 tablespoons tomato paste
2 tablespoons Sherry
4 teaspoons oriental sesame oil
4 teaspoons hoisin sauce
1 tablespoon sugar
2 teaspoons Sherry vinegar

Crush all but 2 tablespoons sesame seed in processor using on/off turns; do not powder. Transfer to nonaluminum bowl. Stir in reserved sesame seed and all remaining ingredients. *(Can be prepared 2 days ahead and refrigerated.)* Serve sauce at room temperature.

Oriental Noodles

6 servings

1 12-ounce package Japanese-style water noodles *(udon)*
¼ cup vegetable oil

18 large green onions including tops (18 ounces total), trimmed and cut into processor feed tube lengths
1 6-ounce can whole water chestnuts, drained, opposite ends cut flat
¼ cup toasted sesame seed
1 teaspoon ground coriander
½ teaspoon salt
¼ cup chicken stock

Bring 2 quarts water to boil in 6-quart saucepan over medium-high heat. Meanwhile, rinse noodles under cold running water until all of potato starch coating is removed. Add noodles to boiling water and bring to boil, stirring frequently to separate. Pour in ½ cup cold water. Return to boil, stirring frequently. Repeat three times, adding ½ cup cold water each time. Continue cooking, stirring frequently, until noodles are tender, about 5 minutes. Drain and rinse noodles under cold running water. Drain again. Combine noodles and ¼ cup oil in saucepan and toss.

Using food processor fitted with medium slicer, place green onions vertically in feed tube and slice using light pressure. Stack water chestnuts in feed tube flat side down and slice using medium pressure. Add onion and water chestnuts to noodles. Add sesame seed, coriander and salt and toss well. Add stock and cook, stirring gently, over medium heat until warmed through. Serve immediately.

Szechuan Dan Dan Noodle

8 to 10 servings

½ cup plus 2 tablespoons chunky peanut butter
5 tablespoons vegetable oil heated with ¼ teaspoon crushed red pepper flakes
3 to 4 tablespoons minced green onion
3 tablespoons soy sauce
2 tablespoons rice vinegar
1 to 2 teaspoons crushed garlic
1 teaspoon sugar
¼ teaspoon crushed Szechuan peppercorns

1 pound Chinese egg noodles
1 bunch spinach or watercress, parboiled and drained

Combine first 8 ingredients in small bowl; add water to thin if necessary.

Cook noodles in boiling water until tender but still firm, checking frequently to avoid overcooking. Drain and transfer to serving bowl. Add spinach and sauce, toss lightly and serve.

Jerry Friedman

Salsa Verde with fettuccine; Shrimp and Feta Cheese Sauce à la Grecque with spaghetti

Stuffed Rotolo

Brian Leatart

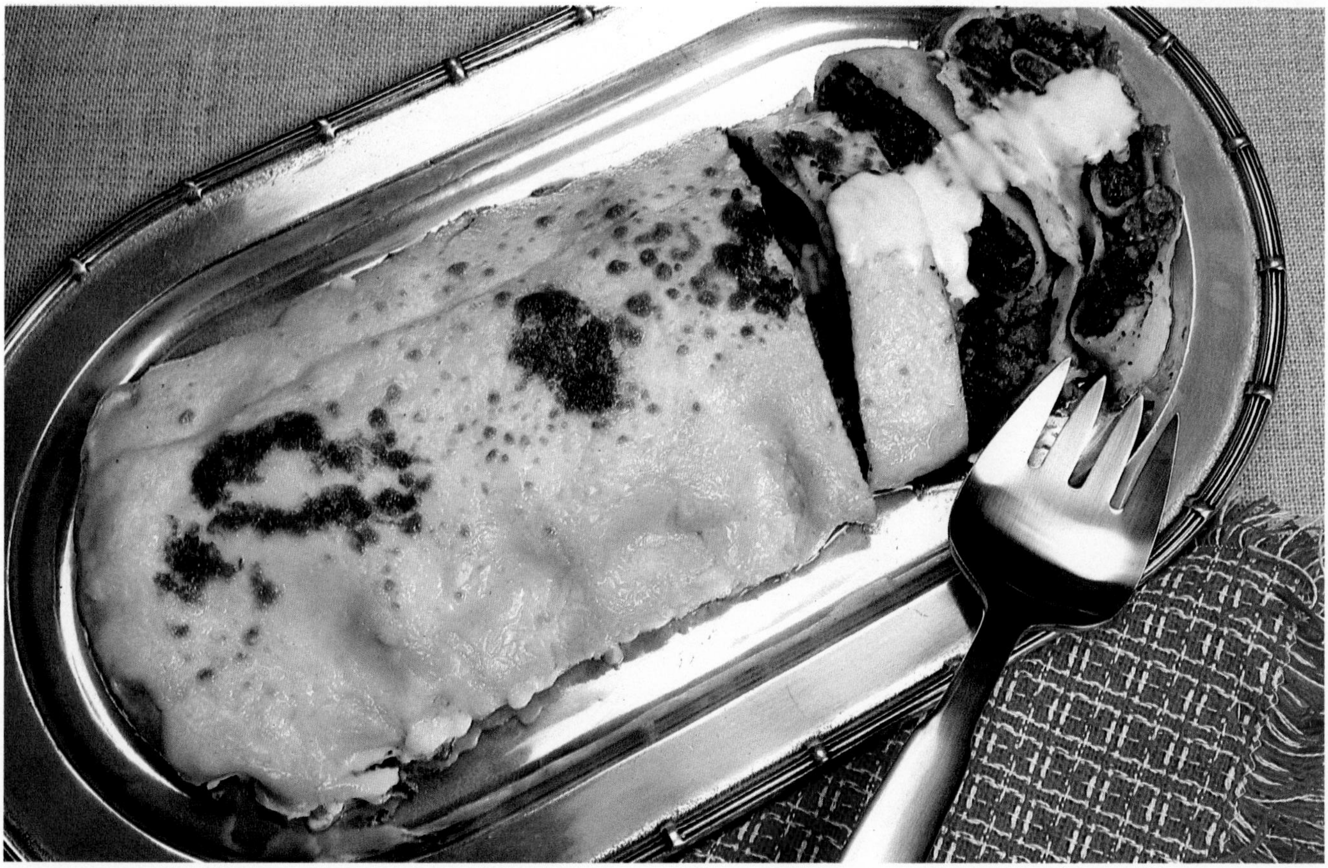

Brian Leatart

Golden Chicken with Saffron Pasta

Brian Leatart

Pappardelle with Rabbit Sauce

Cheese and Tomato Pizza di Bufalo topped with pepperoni, black olives, green pepper and fresh mushrooms

Irwin Horowitz

Dan Wolfe

Red Pepper and Italian Sausage Pizza

Irwin Horowitz

Fruited Cheese Pizza

Marinated Chinese Noodles and Vegetables

Make this salad one day ahead to allow all of the flavors to mellow.

8 servings

Marinade

- 1/2 cup vegetable oil
- 1/2 cup white rice vinegar
- 1/4 cup soy sauce
- 1 tablespoon plus 1 teaspoon sugar
- 2 teaspoons dry mustard
- 1 1/4 teaspoons salt
- 1 teaspoon peanut butter
- 1 teaspoon oriental sesame oil
- 1 teaspoon ground ginger
- Freshly ground pepper

Salad

- 6 quarts water
- 2 tablespoons salt
- 12 ounces oriental dried noodles
- 10 dried black Chinese mushrooms
- 16 fresh snow peas, halved diagonally
- 1 large red bell pepper, seeded and cut into 2-inch rectangles
- 4 large green onions, including tops, cut into 2-inch strips
- 1 large jícama* (21 ounces), peeled and cut into feed-tube lengths
- 4 large carrots (12 ounces total), cut into feed-tube lengths
- 1/4 cup sesame seed (garnish)
- Red bell pepper strips (garnish)

For marinade: Combine all ingredients in food processor fitted with steel knife and mix 2 seconds.

For salad: Bring water to boil with salt in large pot. Add noodles and cook until soft, about 7 minutes. Drain well. Run under cold water to stop cooking process and drain again. Transfer noodles to large bowl. Pour marinade over top and toss thoroughly.

Soak mushrooms in small bowl with enough warm water to cover for 30 minutes. Drain well. Discard stems; slice caps in half. Stir mushroom caps and snow peas into noodles.

Insert thin slicer into processor. Stand red pepper in feed tube and slice using light pressure. Add to noodles. Stack green onions horizontally in feed tube and slice using light pressure. Blend into noodles.

Insert medium slicer. Place jícama in feed tube and slice using medium pressure. Add to noodles. Stack carrots horizontally in feed tube and slice using medium pressure. Add to noodles and toss well. Cover tightly and refrigerate.

Preheat oven to 350°F. Spread sesame seed on baking sheet and bake until golden, about 15 minutes. Let cool.

Bring salad to room temperature. Toss well, taste and adjust seasoning. Cross several red pepper strips decoratively over salad to garnish. Sprinkle sesame seed over top and serve.

*If jícama is unavailable, substitute an equal weight of carrots.

Oriental Pasta Salad Cafe Mariposa

This pretty salad features marinated duck. Everything except the pasta can be prepared one day ahead.

4 to 6 servings

- 1 4 1/2- to 5-pound duck

Oriental Sauce

- 1 cup unseasoned rice vinegar
- 1/2 cup *mirin* (sweet rice wine)
- 1/2 cup soy sauce
- 1/2 cup sugar
- 1/2 onion, sliced
- 1 tablespoon grated fresh ginger
- 2 garlic cloves, minced
- 1/2 teaspoon dried red pepper flakes
- 8 ounces snow peas, strings removed, cut into julienne
- 2 large carrots, peeled and cut into julienne
- 1 pound fresh linguine
- 1/4 cup oriental sesame oil
- 8 ounces zucchini, cut into julienne
- 1/4 cup julienne of pickled ginger *(amazu shoga)*
- 1 red bell pepper, seeded and diced
- Toasted sesame seed

Bring water to boil in bottom of steamer. Arrange duck on steamer rack. Cover and steam until tender, adding more boiling water as necessary, about 1½ hours. Cool to room temperature. Skin and bone duck. Cut meat into julienne; transfer to bowl.

For sauce: Cook first 8 ingredients in heavy small saucepan over low heat, swirling pan occasionally, until sugar dissolves. Increase heat and boil 2 minutes. Strain sauce and cool. Mix 1¼ cups sauce with duck. Reserve remaining sauce. Marinate duck at room temperature 3 hours, turning occasionally.

Blanch snow peas in large pot of boiling salted water until bright green, about 5 seconds. Remove with slotted spoon and drain. Blanch carrots until crisp-tender, about 30 seconds. Drain.

Cook pasta in large pot of boiling salted water, stirring to prevent sticking, until just tender but firm to bite. Drain thoroughly; transfer to large bowl. Combine remaining oriental sauce and sesame oil. Add to pasta and toss. Cool to lukewarm or room temperature. Add snow peas, carrots, zucchini and ginger. Drain duck and add to pasta. Toss to mix well. Arrange on plates. Top with bell pepper and sesame seed and serve.

Chicken and Buckwheat Noodles in Peanut Sauce

Noodles turn up, to the delight of most of us, in almost all cuisines. Here, Japanese buckwheat noodles (soba) *are combined with chicken shreds in a thick, slightly sweet-hot garlic dressing of Southeast Asian descent. If there isn't a local oriental market for the noodles, some health food stores also carry them. Drink an aromatic Thai or Japanese beer with this. If you care to serve a first course, try chilled cucumber soup. Follow this hearty salad with lemon or pineapple ice and a glass of iced mint tea.*

6 servings

3 pounds chicken thighs and legs (about 4 cups cooked chicken)
1 carrot, cut into chunks
1 celery stalk, sliced

½ cup water
⅓ cup soy sauce
2 tablespoons firmly packed dark brown sugar
1 tablespoon grated fresh ginger
1½ teaspoons ground coriander
1 teaspoon grated lemon peel

2 tablespoons peanut oil
⅓ cup sliced green onion
2 to 3 tiny dried hot peppers, seeded and chopped, or ¼ teaspoon red pepper flakes
1½ teaspoons minced garlic
⅓ cup roasted unsalted peanuts
¼ cup fresh lemon juice

7 ounces buckwheat noodles or linguine

2 tablespoons rice vinegar
1 teaspoon sugar
⅛ teaspoon salt
4 cups torn fresh spinach leaves
1 small hot red pepper (optional)

Combine chicken, carrot and celery in large saucepan or Dutch oven with enough lightly salted water to cover. Bring to boiling point over high heat, then reduce heat and simmer gently 20 to 25 minutes. Remove from heat and cool chicken in broth. Discard skin and bone and tear chicken into fine slivers. Transfer to bowl, cover and chill.

Combine next 6 ingredients in small saucepan and blend well. Place over medium-high heat and bring to boil. Remove from heat and set aside.

Heat oil in small skillet over medium-high heat. Add onion, peppers and garlic and sauté until lightly colored. Transfer to food processor or blender and add peanuts and soy sauce mixture. Blend until very smooth. Press through fine sieve into small saucepan. Bring to boil, stirring constantly, then reduce heat and simmer 2 minutes. Cool slightly and stir in lemon juice.

Cook noodles in boiling water until just tender. Drain well and transfer to mixing bowl. Add half of peanut sauce and toss lightly. Add remaining sauce to chicken and blend well. *Salad may be prepared 1 day ahead to this point.*

To serve, combine vinegar, sugar and salt in mixing bowl and blend well. Add spinach and toss thoroughly. Arrange around edge of large deep platter. Pile noodles in center and top with chicken. Slice pepper into flowerlike shape and remove seeds. Place on chicken.

Filipino Chicken with Rice Noodles (Pancit)

8 to 10 servings

3 chicken breast halves, skinned
3 cups water
1/2 teaspoon salt

4 ounces bean threads

1/4 cup (1/2 stick) butter
3 garlic cloves, minced
1 1/2 cups chopped onion
1/2 cup thinly sliced Chinese sausage
1/4 cup soy sauce

8 ounces dried rice noodles

4 celery stalks, cut into julienne (about 3 1/2 cups)
3 medium carrots, cut into julienne (about 2 cups)
5 to 6 medium mushrooms, sliced (about 1/2 cup)
Salt and freshly ground pepper
Sliced hard-cooked egg (garnish)

Combine chicken, water and salt in small saucepan over medium-low heat and poach gently just until cooked, about 12 minutes. Strain, reserving 2 1/2 cups broth. Cool chicken, bone and cut into bite-size pieces.

Meanwhile, soak bean threads in warm water until soft, about 10 minutes. Drain and cut into small pieces. Pat dry.

Melt butter in wok or very large skillet over medium heat. Add garlic and sauté just until brown; do not burn. Add onion, sausage and soy sauce. Cover and simmer 10 minutes. Add reserved chicken broth and bean threads and bring to boil.

Meanwhile, soak rice noodles in water just until soft, about 3 to 4 minutes; do not oversoak. Drain well in colander.

Add rice noodles, celery, carrot and mushrooms to onion mixture. Increase heat to medium-high and cook, stirring constantly, until broth evaporates, about 5 to 8 minutes. Add chicken. Season to taste with salt and pepper. Transfer to heated large dish. Garnish with sliced cooked egg and serve.

Cold Noodles with Peanut Butter Sauce

This salad would make a special lunch treat. Many of the components can be made the day before serving.

4 main-course servings or 6 servings as part of multi-course Chinese meal

8 ounces skinned and boned chicken breast
3/4 teaspoon cornstarch
1 1/4 teaspoons oriental sesame oil
1/2 teaspoon salt
1/8 teaspoon freshly ground white pepper

5 ounces Chinese-style dried egg noodles
2 1/2 tablespoons vegetable oil

2 eggs

Peanut Butter Sauce
5 tablespoons water
3 tablespoons creamy peanut butter
1 1/2 tablespoons distilled white vinegar
1 tablespoon soy sauce
1 teaspoon Chinese chili oil
1/4 teaspoon salt

6 ounces bean sprouts, trimmed

2 ounces Black Forest ham, cut into 1/10 × 1-inch strips
1 medium cucumber, peeled, seeded and cut into 1/10 × 1-inch strips
Green onion slivers

Cut chicken with grain into 1/10 × 1/10 × 1-inch strips. Place in small bowl with cornstarch, 1/4 teaspoon sesame oil, 1/4 teaspoon salt and 1/8 teaspoon pepper. Marinate 30 minutes at room temperature. *(Can be prepared 1 day ahead. Cover and refrigerate.)*

Add noodles to large pot of rapidly boiling water, stirring to prevent sticking. Cook until just firm but almost tender (al dente), about 4 minutes. Rinse with cold water 30 seconds. Drain thoroughly. Transfer to bowl. Toss with 1 tablespoon vegetable oil and 1 teaspoon sesame oil. Cool 30 minutes. *(Can be prepared 1 day ahead. Cover and refrigerate.)*

Beat eggs to blend with ¼ teaspoon salt. Heat wok or heavy 8-inch skillet over high heat 45 seconds. Add ½ tablespoon vegetable oil and heat 30 seconds. Pour in eggs and tilt pan to spread to 8-inch diameter. Cook until top is almost set, about 1½ minutes. Turn and cook 30 seconds. Remove from pan. Cool 15 minutes. Cut into $\frac{1}{10} \times 1$-inch strips. *(Can be prepared 1 day ahead. Cover and refrigerate.)*

For sauce: Gradually mix water into peanut butter in serving bowl and stir until smooth. Blend in vinegar, soy sauce, chili oil and salt. *(Can be prepared 3 hours ahead. Stir before using.)*

Heat wok over high heat 30 seconds. Add remaining 1 tablespoon vegetable oil and heat 30 seconds. Add chicken and stir-fry until just white, about 1½ minutes. Remove from wok and cool.

Blanch bean sprouts in large amount of boiling water 3 seconds. Drain.

Just before serving, toss noodles lightly and transfer to platter or large bowl. Spoon bean sprouts in center of noodles. Arrange ham, egg, chicken and cucumber in concentric circles around sprouts. Garnish with green onions. Pass sauce separately.

Balinese Fried Noodles (Bakmi Goreng)

6 servings

¼ cup peanut oil
1 large garlic clove, minced

4 ounces cooked small shrimp
1 cup shredded cooked chicken
1 pound Chinese egg noodles, cooked and drained
1 cup shredded bok choy
2 tablespoons Indonesian soy sauce or Kecap Manis*

1 tablespoon peanut oil
1 large sweet onion, minced

1 tablespoon unsalted butter
2 eggs

Heat ¼ cup oil in wok or very large skillet over medium heat. Add garlic and sauté about 1 minute. Add shrimp and chicken and stir-fry 3 minutes. Add noodles, bok choy and soy sauce and cook, stirring and tossing, until noodles are heated through, about 3 to 5 minutes. Cover and keep warm.

Heat remaining oil in small skillet over high heat. Add onion and fry until well browned and slightly crisp but not burned; keep warm.

Melt butter in skillet over medium heat. Add eggs and scramble lightly.

Divide noodles among heated plates and top with scrambled egg and onion. Serve immediately.

*Kecap Manis (Indonesian Soy Sauce)

A common ingredient in Balinese and Indonesian cuisine. If commercial Kecap Manis is not readily available in your area, use this recipe.

Makes about 3 cups

1 cup firmly packed dark brown sugar
1 cup water
1 cup Japanese soy sauce
7 tablespoons dark molasses
1 teaspoon grated fresh ginger
½ teaspoon ground coriander
½ teaspoon freshly ground pepper

Combine sugar and water in 2-quart saucepan. Bring to simmer over medium heat, stirring just until sugar dissolves. Increase heat to high and continue cooking until syrup reaches 200°F on candy thermometer, about 5 minutes. Reduce heat to low, stir in remaining ingredients and simmer 3 minutes.

Kecap Manis will keep 2 to 3 months tightly covered and stored in refrigerator.

Stir-Fried Transparent Noodles (Sotanghon)

Annatto seed imparts a brilliant orange color to this dish. Leftover beef can be added just before serving.

12 servings

1 8.8-ounce package bean thread vermicelli*

2 tablespoons annatto seed**
1/2 cup dried shiitake mushrooms

5 tablespoons vegetable oil
10 medium garlic cloves, coarsely crushed in mortar with pestle
1 1-pound chicken breast, skinned, boned and cut into 1/2-inch cubes
1 cup thinly sliced green onions
2 Chinese sausages, cut into 1/4-inch cubes
1 cup peeled and deveined small shrimp
2 cups rich chicken stock
1/4 cup fish sauce *(patis)***

Soak vermicelli in cold water to cover for 1 hour or overnight.

Soak annatto seed in 1/2 cup water 45 minutes. Soak shiitake mushrooms in warm water to cover until softened, about 30 minutes. Drain mushrooms, squeeze out excess moisture and cut into 1/8-inch slices, discarding stems.

Drain vermicelli; cut into 4-inch lengths. Heat oil in wok or heavy large skillet over high heat. Add garlic and stir-fry until golden. Remove garlic and reserve. Add chicken, shiitake mushrooms and 1/2 cup green onions to wok and stir-fry 1 minute. Add Chinese sausages and shrimp and stir-fry until shrimp just turns opaque, about 1 1/2 minutes. Transfer mixture to bowl using slotted spoon. Bring stock and fish sauce to boil in wok. Strain annatto soaking liquid into wok through fine sieve. Submerge sieve in boiling broth, crushing seed against sieve to release more color. Discard seed. Mix vermicelli into liquid. Simmer until liquid is absorbed, about 10 minutes, stirring frequently and returning shrimp mixture to wok for last 1 minute to reheat. Transfer noodle mixture to large platter. Top with remaining 1/2 cup green onions. Sprinkle with browned garlic or pass separately. Serve noodles immediately.

*Transparent noodles made from mung beans.

**Also called achiote seed, these small red seeds are available at Filipino, Latin American and Spanish markets. The fish sauce is available at Filipino markets.

Fried Rice Noodles with Barbecued Pork

8 to 12 servings

4 tablespoons vegetable oil
4 small onions, thinly sliced
2 large garlic cloves, minced
2 fresh red chilies, seeded and chopped, or 2 fresh green hot chilies mixed with a little chopped red bell pepper
8 ounces Barbecued Pork,* thinly sliced
8 ounces uncooked shrimp, shelled and deveined
8 ounces cleaned squid (optional; use additional 8 ounces shrimp, if preferred)
3 or 4 Chinese pork sausages, steamed and thinly sliced
1 cup fresh bean sprouts, ends pinched off

2 pounds fresh rice noodles, cut into 1/4-inch-wide strips
2 tablespoons dark soy sauce
2 tablespoons light soy sauce
1 tablespoon oyster sauce
3 eggs, beaten
Salt and freshly ground pepper
4 green onions, chopped (garnish)

Heat 2 tablespoons oil in wok over medium heat. Add onion, garlic and chilies and stir-fry until tender. Add pork, shrimp, squid and sausage and stir-fry over high heat until seafood is cooked, 2 to 3 minutes. Add bean sprouts; toss lightly. Remove from wok.

Heat remaining oil in wok. Add noodles and stir-fry until very hot, 2 to 3 minutes. Add soy and oyster sauces and mix well. Stirring constantly, add beaten egg and cook until set. Return first mixture to wok and toss to mix well. Taste and season with salt and pepper. Turn onto platter and garnish with chopped green onion.

*Barbecued Pork

1 12- to 15-ounce pork tenderloin, well trimmed
2 tablespoons hoisin sauce
1½ tablespoons catsup
1 garlic clove, mashed
1 tablespoon dark soy sauce
2 teaspoons Shaohsing*
1½ teaspoons light soy sauce
½ teaspoon sugar

Place pork on plate. Combine remaining ingredients and spread over meat. Cover and chill overnight.

Preheat oven to 350°F. Set pork on rack over shallow pan and roast 45 minutes, brushing several times with sauce.

*Chinese rice wine; Sherry can be substituted.

Thai Fried Noodles (Pad Thai)

4 servings

2 whole large chicken breasts, skinned, boned and cut crosswise into ¼-inch-thick slices (about 2 pounds total)
2 tablespoons Sherry

2 tablespoons vegetable oil
¼ cup fresh basil leaves

3 tablespoons vegetable oil
8 medium garlic cloves, thinly sliced (1 ounce total)
6 medium shallots, peeled and slivered lengthwise (3 ounces total)
12 ounces rice-stick or rice vermicelli noodles, soaked in hot water 15 minutes and drained

4 red serrano chilies, seeded and chopped, or 4 dried red chilies, seeded and chopped
1 teaspoon shrimp paste *(kapee)* or anchovy paste
½ teaspoon salt
1 tablespoon vegetable oil
6 dried oriental mushrooms, soaked in hot water until soft, hard cores discarded and caps sliced
6 ounces cooked small shrimp, shelled and squeezed dry in paper towels
3 tablespoons tomato paste
2 tablespoons sugar
1 tablespoon fish sauce *(nam pla)*
½ cup bean sprouts (about 1 ounce)
¼ cup fresh basil leaves
2 tablespoons roasted peanuts, coarsely pounded
½ teaspoon dried red pepper flakes
4 cherry tomatoes, each cut almost through into 8 wedges (garnish)

Combine chicken with Sherry in small bowl; marinate at least 30 minutes.

Heat 2 tablespoons oil in small skillet over medium-high heat. Add basil leaves and stir-fry briefly until crisp. Drain on paper towels; set aside.

Heat 3 tablespoons oil in small skillet over medium heat. Add garlic and shallot and fry until crisp. Remove garlic and shallot using slotted spoon and set aside. Pour oil into large bowl. Add noodles and toss gently to coat.

Combine chilies, shrimp paste and salt in mortar and pound until smooth. Heat remaining 1 tablespoon oil in wok over high heat. Add chili paste and stir-fry until aroma mellows, about 1 minute. Add mushrooms with chicken mixture and stir-fry 3 minutes.

Add shrimp and cook just until heated through. Blend in tomato paste, sugar and fish sauce. Add bean sprouts and 1/4 cup fresh basil leaves and stir-fry 2 minutes. Add noodles in 3 batches, tossing gently after each addition until thoroughly coated and heated through. Transfer to serving platter. Sprinkle with fried basil leaves, peanuts, pepper flakes and reserved garlic and shallot. Garnish with cherry tomatoes. Serve immediately.

Cantonese Seafood Noodle

This well-seasoned dish contrasts succulent seafood and crisp vegetables with noodles that are crisp outside and tender inside. Can be served as dim sum or as a one-dish meal.

2 main-course servings; up to 6 servings with other dishes

2 tablespoons peanut oil
1 teaspoon oriental sesame oil
1/4 teaspoon salt
1/4 teaspoon freshly ground white pepper

1 1/2 teaspoons minced fresh ginger
1 1/2 teaspoons minced garlic
2 1/2 tablespoons light soy sauce
2 1/2 tablespoons Shaohsing*
1 cup chicken stock
1 tablespoon plus 2 teaspoons oyster sauce
1/2 teaspoon sugar
1/4 teaspoon freshly ground white pepper

3 to 4 cleaned squid (optional), tentacles discarded

1 quart (4 cups) water
1/4 cup Chinese broccoli stalks cut into 1 1/2-inch lengths or peeled broccoli (if stalks are larger than 1/2 inch in diameter, split in half)
4 quarts water

8 ounces fresh or dried Chinese egg noodles

4 tablespoons peanut oil

3 cups peanut oil
1/3 cup uncooked shelled shrimp, cut in half lengthwise (about 3 large shrimp)
1/3 cup sea scallops sliced into discs 1/4 inch thick (about 3 scallops)

1/4 cup celery cut into 1 1/2 × 1/4-inch julienne
6 small dried Chinese black mushrooms, soaked 30 minutes in water, drained, stems discarded, caps sliced
1/4 cup green onion tops cut into 1 1/2-inch lengths
3/4 teaspoon oriental sesame oil
1 tablespoon cornstarch dissolved in 3 tablespoons water

Combine 2 tablespoons peanut oil, 1 teaspoon sesame oil, salt and 1/4 teaspoon white pepper in small bowl; set aside.

Combine ginger and garlic. Combine soy sauce and wine in small bowl. Mix stock, oyster sauce, sugar and remaining pepper in another bowl. Set aside.

Split squid almost through lengthwise. Score inside of squid in both directions at 1/8-inch intervals, cutting diagonally at 45-degree angle so it is crosshatched. Following scoring lines, cut squid into 1 1/2-inch pieces.

Bring 1 quart water to boil in wok or saucepan. Add broccoli and blanch about 1 minute. Drain, rinse with cold water and drain again. Set aside. Bring 4 quarts water to boil in wok or saucepan. Add noodles and boil until al dente. Drain. Toss with oil mixture.

Heat 3 tablespoons peanut oil in 10-inch skillet until very hot. Add noodles as solid mass (do not separate) and cook until golden brown on bottom, about

5 minutes. Invert onto plate. Add 1 tablespoon oil to skillet and heat until very hot. Return noodles browned side up. Cook, shaking pan frequently, until bottom is golden brown, about 4 minutes. Transfer to platter; keep warm.

Heat 3 cups peanut oil in wok to 225°F. Add shrimp and cook until they turn pink. Remove with slotted spoon and drain. Add scallops and cook until they just turn white. Remove with slotted spoon, drain and add to shrimp. Add squid to wok and cook until they curl into roll. Remove with slotted spoon, drain and add to shrimp and scallops.

Discard all but 3 tablespoons oil; strain and return to wok. Heat oil again. Add ginger and garlic mixture and stir-fry 10 seconds. Add celery and broccoli and stir-fry 10 seconds. Add mushrooms and stir-fry 5 seconds. Add seafood mixture and stir-fry 5 seconds. Add green onion tops and mix well. Add combined wine and soy sauce and mix well. Add broth mixture and bring to simmer. Stir in sesame oil. Add dissolved cornstarch and stir-fry until sauce thickens. Taste and adjust seasoning. Pour over noodles and serve.

*Chinese rice wine; Sherry can be substituted.

7 Pizza

Pizza! From streetcorner eateries in Brooklyn to chic *nouvelle* establishments on the West Coast, it's everyone's favorite: There is something irresistible about that combination of crisp crust and rich, savory topping.

Like pasta, pizza is booming lately. No longer an unvarying combination of tomato sauce and mozzarella, pizza now appears with exciting new toppings that would have been unimaginable just a few years ago.

This chapter will give you a good hint of the possibilities: There are two Mexican-style versions (pages 107 and 109), Pizza Niçoise (page 104), Mushroom Pizza with Garlic Butter (page 98) and plenty of others. For those who just can't get enough, the chapter concludes with a dessert pizza crowned by orange-scented cheese and fresh fruit.

Since the foundation of good pizza is a good crust, the chapter includes a detailed Pizza Primer that will tell you everything you need to know about equipment and procedures. Take careful note of the instructions for mixing, shaping and baking the dough; they include some professional tricks that will give you truly impressive results.

Shaping a round of pizza dough by tossing it aloft is a thrill that few culinary tasks can match. Once you have mastered the process, you will find pizza every bit as much fun to make as it is to serve.

Mushroom Pizza with Garlic Butter

Makes one 12-inch pizza

Basic Pizza Dough for 12-inch pizza (see page 101)

1 medium tomato (about 6 to 7 ounces), peeled, seeded, juiced and coarsely chopped
3/4 teaspoon salt

1/4 cup (1/2 stick) butter
1 tablespoon minced shallot
2 teaspoons minced garlic

10 ounces mushrooms
4 ounces freshly grated Italian Bel Paese cheese (about 1 cup)
1 tablespoon minced fresh parsley
1 1/2 teaspoons minced fresh tarragon or thyme or 1/2 teaspoon dried, crumbled

3 ounces pancetta, minced*

Olive oil
1/4 cup freshly grated Romano or Parmesan cheese

2 tablespoons freshly grated Parmesan cheese
1 1/2 tablespoons minced fresh chives

Prepare basic dough. Set aside to rise.

Place tomato in colander. Sprinkle with salt and let drain at least 30 minutes. Squeeze until completely dry (potato ricer works well). Roll tightly in cheesecloth or kitchen towel.

Combine butter, shallot and garlic in small saucepan and place over low heat until butter is melted. Cool 10 minutes.

Clean mushrooms with damp paper towel; *do not rinse or pizza will be soggy.* Slice thinly, then extract liquid by squeezing one handful of mushrooms at a time in potato ricer or corner of dishcloth. Transfer to bowl. Add melted butter mixture and toss lightly. Stir in Bel Paese, parsley and tarragon.

Cook pancetta in heavy small saucepan over low heat, stirring occasionally, until fat is rendered and pancetta is lightly browned. Remove from pan using slotted spoon. Add to mushroom mixture and stir gently.

Position rack in center of oven and arrange baking stone or quarry tiles over top. Preheat oven to 425°F for 30 minutes. Shape pizza dough into 12-inch circle following Basic Pizza Dough directions. Brush with olive oil. Sprinkle with Romano or Parmesan cheese and top with mushroom mixture, leaving 1/2-inch border. Bake until crust browns, about 15 to 20 minutes.

Brush rim of pizza with olive oil. If mushrooms release liquid during cooking, pierce rim of pizza with sharp knife, then tilt to drain liquid through slit. Starting at slit, divide pizza into serving pieces with pizza cutter, scissors or serrated knife. Sprinkle with Parmesan and chives. Serve immediately.

*Prosciutto or other ham can be substituted for pancetta; do not cook first. If prosciutto is used, reduce salt to 1/2 teaspoon.

Easy Italian Pizza

4 servings

1 13 3/4-ounce package hot roll mix
1 8-ounce can tomato sauce
1 garlic clove, minced
2 tablespoons tomato paste
1 teaspoon Italian herb seasoning
12 ounces mozzarella cheese, shredded
1 green bell pepper, seeded and chopped
1 onion, thinly sliced
Thinly sliced pepperoni or other ready-to-eat sausage
Sliced olives
Anchovy fillets

Preheat oven to 450°F. Follow package directions for mixing and baking 14-inch pizza crust. Meanwhile, combine next 4 ingredients in small saucepan over medium-high heat and bring to boil, stirring constantly. Reduce heat and simmer about 10 minutes. Spread sauce evenly over baked crust and sprinkle with cheese. Arrange remaining ingredients over top. Bake until cheese is melted, about 20 minutes. Cut into wedges and serve.

Pizza Anchoiade with Mortadella and Olives

Makes one 12-inch pizza

Basic Pizza Dough for 12-inch pizza (see page 101)

1¾ pounds tomatoes (preferably Italian pear tomatoes), peeled, seeded, juiced and finely chopped
1½ teaspoons salt

2 tablespoons olive oil
1 small onion, thinly sliced

2 large garlic cloves
6 anchovy fillets (or more to taste)
3 tablespoons olive oil

2 tablespoons *each* freshly grated Parmesan and Romano cheese
5 ounces buffalo milk mozzarella, sliced (about 1¼ cups), or 2½ ounces *each* freshly grated mozzarella cheese (preferably whole milk) and Italian Fontina cheese
Freshly ground pepper
4 slices mortadella or 8 slices Italian salami, quartered
16 Niçoise olives, pitted and halved

Olive oil
2 tablespoons freshly grated Romano cheese
2 tablespoons minced fresh basil, thyme, marjoram or oregano

Prepare basic dough. Set aside to rise.

Place tomatoes in colander. Sprinkle with salt and let drain at least 30 minutes. Squeeze until completely dry (potato ricer works well). Roll tightly in cheesecloth or kitchen towel to remove any remaining moisture.

Heat 2 tablespoons olive oil in heavy small skillet over low heat. Add onion. Cover and cook, stirring occasionally, until translucent, about 10 minutes.

Crush garlic to paste in mortar. Add anchovies and continue mashing until pureed. Whisk in 3 tablespoons olive oil 1 tablespoon at a time.

Position rack in center of oven and arrange baking stone or quarry tiles over top. Preheat oven to 425°F for 30 minutes. Shape pizza dough into 12-inch circle following Basic Pizza Dough directions. Brush with garlic-anchovy paste, leaving ½-inch border. Layer dough with Parmesan, Romano, half of mozzarella, all of tomatoes and sautéed onion. Sprinkle lightly with pepper and top with remaining mozzarella. Bake 15 minutes. Arrange mortadella and olives over top. Bake until crust browns, about 5 more minutes.

Brush rim of pizza with olive oil. If tomatoes release liquid during cooking, pierce rim of pizza, then tilt to drain liquid through slit. Starting at slit, divide pizza into serving pieces with pizza cutter, scissors or serrated knife. Sprinkle with remaining 2 tablespoons Romano and basil. Serve hot.

Pizza Primer

Equipment

Your homemade pizzas will be best if you cook them on a ceramic baking stone. Available at cookware stores or through mail order, these porous trays simulate old-fashioned brick ovens. While they may not attain the high temperatures of Neapolitan furnaces manufactured from Mount Vesuvius's black volcanic rock, they retain enough heat to draw out the dough's moisture and produce a delicious crackling crust. Marketed in 12- and 16-inch rounds, a 14- to 16-inch rectangle and a 10-inch deep-dish pan for Sicilian pies, the stones can also be utilized for bread, cookies and tart shells.

Although less expensive half-inch-thick unglazed quarry tiles can be substituted for baking stones, they do not produce a crust as crisp as one made on a baking stone, and their seams make it difficult to slide pizzas on and off them. A long-handled wooden baker's peel facilitates this task; a plywood board or flat cookie sheet will work but they don't *feel* as professional.

Ingredients

Today's home pizza maker can take advantage of the wide range of foodstuffs that has become available recently: extra virgin olive oil, vine-ripened tomatoes, exotic mushrooms, fine imported hams and sausages and an ever-increasing supply of cheeses from Lombardy and Sicily. But don't limit yourself to thinking Italian. Possibilities for toppings are endless.

No matter what their ethnicity, fresh uncooked ingredients give pizza the most pizzazz. Anything that exudes liquid should be dried well before cooking; if liquid still escapes, remove it with a bulb baster or drain it through a slit cut in the crust. When layering ingredients, place some of the cheese on the bottom to keep the crust crisp. Foods that need to be moistened while cooking—fish and onions, for example—should be placed under tomatoes; foods requiring the most heat, such as sausage, should be put on top. Mozzarella, particularly the skim milk variety, gives pizza its characteristic long strands, but its rubbery texture can be modified by substituting some Italian Fontina, Bel Paese or other good melting cheese. Another alternative is to use buffalo milk mozzarella: Its clean tart flavor adds a superb touch.

Topping ingredients, like those for stir-fry, can be cut and readied ahead.

Any leftover uncooked dough can be baked for bread or added to the next batch of homemade pizza dough.

Basic Pizza Dough

4 first-course or 2 main-course servings

Dough for 12-inch pizza

- 1½ cups bread flour or all purpose flour
- ½ teaspoon salt
- ¾ teaspoon dry yeast
- ½ cup to ½ cup plus 1 tablespoon warm water (105°F to 115°F)
- 1 tablespoon olive oil
- Rice flour or all purpose flour
- Cornmeal

6 to 8 first-course or 3 to 4 main-course servings

Dough for 14-inch pizza

- 2 cups bread flour or all purpose flour
- ¾ teaspoon salt
- 1 teaspoon dry yeast
- ⅔ cup to ⅔ cup plus 1 tablespoon warm water (105°F to 115°F)
- 1 tablespoon olive oil
- Rice flour or all purpose flour
- Cornmeal

8 to 10 first-course or 4 to 5 main-course servings

Dough for 16-inch pizza

- 2½ cups bread flour or all purpose flour
- 1 teaspoon salt
- 1½ teaspoons dry yeast
- ¾ cup to ¾ cup plus 2 tablespoons warm water (105°F to 115°F)
- 2 tablespoons olive oil
- Rice flour or all purpose flour
- Cornmeal

Mixing

This dough can be prepared several days ahead and allowed to rise before being punched down and refrigerated until two to three hours before shaping and baking. If dough rises before it is needed, punch down and let rise again, or refrigerate up to two days. Bring to room temperature at least two hours before using. When making 14-inch or 16-inch pizzas, increase topping proportions in a 12-inch-pizza recipe by about ⅛ and ¼ respectively.

Here is the point where you can begin giving the pizza your own personal touch. Most basic recipes use ¼-inch crust thickness as a general guide, but alter the dough to suit individual preference. For a thinner, crisper crust, make the dough drier and shape to ⅛-inch thickness, trimming off excess. Increase oven temperature to 475°F or 500°F and bake until brown, about 15 minutes. For a thicker crust, make dough moister and softer. Let rise again 30 minutes before topping.

By hand: Mix flour and salt on work surface or in bowl. Make 5-inch well in center, distributing flour evenly around sides so water does not run out. Sprinkle yeast into well. Pour about 2 tablespoons water into well and mix with fingertips until yeast is dissolved. Pour in remaining water with olive oil. Starting from inside of circle, gradually brush flour into liquid with fingers. When all flour is incorporated, gather dough into ball. Knead until smooth and elastic, occasionally slapping dough forcefully on surface, about 7 to 10 minutes. If any dry particles remain, sprinkle with drops of water. If dough is too sticky, knead in additional flour. Dough should be soft and easy to knead; however, dough becomes softer as it rises and if too soft, it will be difficult to shape.

With food processor: Mix flour and salt in work bowl using several on/off turns. Sprinkle yeast over water and stir until dissolved. Add olive oil to yeast mixture. With machine running, add yeast mixture through feed tube and continue processing until dough is smooth, moist and well mixed, about 7 seconds; *dough should not form ball.* Turn dough out onto work surface and knead until silken, about 3 minutes.

With heavy-duty mixer: Combine flour and salt in large bowl of electric mixer fitted with dough hook. Sprinkle yeast over water and stir until dissolved. Add olive oil to yeast mixture. With machine running at low speed, gradually pour yeast mixture into flour and knead according to manufacturer's instructions until dough has massed on hook and becomes smooth and silken, about 15 to 20 minutes (if dough does not cling to hook after about 5 minutes, beater height may need adjustment; check instruction booklet). If dough starts to climb onto head of mixer, sprinkle with 1 to 2 tablespoons flour to prevent sticking.

Rising

Forming dough into circle for rising makes eventual shaping of pizza easier. To do so, hold dough with left hand while stretching dough towards you and tucking ends underneath with right hand. Turn dough slightly and repeat folding and tucking until ball forms. Pat sides of dough to even ball. Sprinkle ball and baking sheet with rice flour. (Rice flour is preferred because it is not readily absorbed.) Arrange dough tucked side down on sheet. Cover dough completely with plastic wrap to prevent crust from forming, but allowing enough space between dough and wrap for dough to expand. Transfer to cold oven and let rise until dough doubles to triples in volume, about 1½ to 2 hours.

Shaping

Pizza can be shaped successfully with or without tossing. The steps may seem awkward to the beginner on first try, but they are easily mastered.

To shape without tossing: Flour hands lightly. Make 2 fists and fit together under center of dough, forming flat surface for dough to rest on. Gradually pull fists apart, turning them simultaneously, to stretch dough. If dough sticks, flour hands again. As center becomes thin, move fists farther apart to stretch sides of dough. Repeat as necessary, being careful not to make dough too thin in center. Thin out edge by pulling dough between rounded thumb and first finger. Dough should be about ¼ inch thick.

To shape by tossing: Flour hands lightly. Make 2 fists and cross wrists closely together under center of dough. In one smooth motion, stretch dough by pulling fists outward and uncrossing wrists in twisting motion to give dough spin while tossing upward. Catch dough on fists. Flour hands again if dough sticks. Cross wrists lower on forearms (fists will be farther apart so sides of dough will be stretched when tossed). Repeat toss; do not toss more than twice or dough will be too thin in center. Thin out edge by pulling dough between rounded thumb and first finger. Dough should be about ¼ inch thick.

Baking

When baking several pizzas and only one oven is available, prepare the second pizza on another peel to go into the oven when the first one comes out.

Thirty minutes before shaping dough, position rack in center of oven and line with baking stone or quarry tiles. (If using optional steaming method, see additional instructions following.) Preheat oven to 425°F.

Meanwhile, flatten dough into as wide a circle as possible by repeatedly pushing down and out in rocking motion with fingertips (avoid using rolling pin, which compresses dough). If dough is sticky, lightly flour dough and work surface. Turn dough over and repeat procedure on other side until dough measures 8 to 9 inches in diameter.

Sprinkle peel or thin wooden board with cornmeal. Place dough on peel. Shape to correct size. Pinch ends up to form thick edge. Just before baking, place topping on pizza (if added sooner, pizza will be soggy). Shake peel back and forth. If pizza does not move freely, slide long, flexible-blade spatula under dough to loosen. Sprinkle preheated baking stone or quarry tiles with cornmeal. Starting from back of baking stone, tip peel and ease far edge of pizza out onto baking stone, then pull peel quickly out from under pizza, leaving pizza on stone. When pizza is cooked, slip peel under crust and transfer to serving board.

Optional Steaming Method

To further simulate a baker's oven, steam can be added when cooking pizza. Fill broiler pan half full with water and set aside. Place firebrick on floor of oven at same time baking stone is preheated. When oven is ready, set broiler pan on opened oven door. Carefully transfer firebrick to prepared broiler pan using fireplace tongs. Set pan on floor of oven. Close door and let steam develop for several minutes before adding pizza.

Pizza Dough with Starter

Dough for two 15-inch pizzas

This dough variation, a specialty of Berkeley's Chez Panisse restaurant, uses a sponge "starter" that lends lightness to the dough. The rye flour adds an intriguing texture. These two crusts will yield six to eight main-course servings total.

Sponge

1 envelope dry yeast
1/2 cup warm water (105°F to 115°F)
1/2 cup all purpose flour

Dough

12 to 13 tablespoons warm water (105°F to 115°F)
3 tablespoons plus 2 teaspoons olive oil
1 1/2 teaspoons salt
3 1/2 cups all purpose flour
3 tablespoons rye flour

For sponge: Sprinkle yeast over water in large mixing bowl and stir with wooden spatula until dissolved. Blend in flour. Cover bowl with plastic wrap. Transfer to cold oven until mixture expands and is bubbling actively, about 15 minutes to 1 hour.

For dough: Gently fold water, olive oil and salt into sponge. Stir in all purpose and rye flours, mixing well. Turn dough out onto work surface. Knead until dough is smooth and silky, adding more all purpose flour and water drops as needed, about 7 to 10 minutes. Rise and shape according to directions for Basic Pizza Dough.

Shrimp and Leek Pizza with Feta Cheese

Makes one 12-inch pizza

Basic Pizza Dough for 12-inch pizza (see page 101)

1 large tomato (about 8 to 9 ounces), peeled, seeded, juiced and diced
3/4 teaspoon salt

2 tablespoons (1/4 stick) butter
2 tablespoons olive oil
1 1/2 cups thinly sliced leek (white and light green part of 2 medium leeks)
Salt and freshly ground pepper

4 to 6 ounces medium shrimp, shelled, deveined and halved lengthwise
1 1/2 tablespoons olive oil

Olive oil

4 ounces feta cheese, crumbled (about 1 scant cup)
1 ounce freshly grated Gruyère or Emmenthal cheese (about 1/4 cup)

3 tablespoons freshly grated Parmesan cheese
1 1/2 tablespoons minced fresh mint or 2 teaspoons dried, crumbled

Preheat basic dough. Set aside to rise.

Place tomato in colander. Sprinkle with salt and let drain at least 30 minutes. Squeeze until completely dry (potato ricer works well). Roll tightly in cheesecloth or kitchen towel to remove any remaining moisture.

Heat butter and 2 tablespoons oil in heavy small skillet over medium-low heat. Add leek. Cover and cook, stirring occasionally, until tender, about 15 minutes. Season leek with salt and freshly ground pepper to taste.

Combine shrimp and 1 1/2 tablespoons olive oil in small bowl and mix well. Season with salt and pepper to taste. Marinate at room temperature for 15 minutes, stirring occasionally.

Position rack in center of oven and arrange baking stone or quarry tiles over top. Preheat oven to 425°F for 30 minutes. Shape pizza dough into 12-inch circle following Basic Pizza Dough directions. Brush with olive oil. Combine feta and Gruyère and sprinkle over pizza, leaving 1/2-inch border. Top with layer of leek, then tomato. Bake until crust browns, about 15 to 20 minutes. Arrange shrimp on top and continue baking until shrimp turn pink, about 2 to 3 more minutes.

Brush rim of pizza with olive oil. Divide pizza into serving pieces with pizza cutter, scissors or serrated knife. Sprinkle with grated Parmesan cheese and mint. Serve immediately.

Pizza Niçoise

2 servings

1/4 cup olive oil
1 large garlic clove, finely chopped
1 large eggplant (about 12 ounces), cut into 1/2-inch cubes
2 cups peeled, seeded and chopped Italian plum tomatoes or one 16-ounce can plum tomatoes, drained and chopped
12 Niçoise olives, pitted and halved

1 large shaped Pizza Dough circle or 2 small circles (see Red Pepper and Italian Sausage Pizza, page 107)
6 ounces mozzarella cheese, shredded
4 ounces pepperoni, thinly sliced
2 tablespoons olive oil
1 tablespoon chopped fresh oregano or 1 teaspoon dried, crumbled

Preheat oven to 425°F. Heat 1/4 cup olive oil in heavy large skillet over medium-high heat. Add garlic and cook until lightly colored, about 2 minutes. Add eggplant and cook until just tender, stirring frequently, 5 to 6 minutes. Add tomatoes and olives and cook 3 minutes. Cool to room temperature.

Spread eggplant mixture on prepared dough circle(s). Top with mozzarella. Arrange pepperoni slices over cheese. Drizzle with olive oil and sprinkle with oregano. Bake until topping is bubbling and crust is golden brown, 15 to 20 minutes. Cut into wedges and serve.

Cheese and Tomato Pizza di Bufalo

Buffalo milk mozzarella, a spun-curd Italian cheese based on water buffalo milk, is much fresher than factory produced "pizza cheese." Before using, drain and pat it dry with paper towels. If it is not obtainable, substitute a mixture of Italian Fontina and mozzarella. Whole-milk mozzarella is preferable for its exquisite richness, although it means sacrificing the wonderful long strands produced by the skim-milk variety. The amounts of cheese and finely chopped tomato can be varied to suit individual taste.

Makes one 12-inch pizza

Basic Pizza Dough for 12-inch pizza (see page 101)

1 3/4 pounds tomatoes (preferably Italian pear tomatoes), peeled, seeded, juiced and finely chopped (or more to taste)
2 teaspoons salt

Olive oil
1/4 cup freshly grated Parmesan cheese
6 to 8 ounces buffalo milk mozzarella, sliced (about 1 1/2 cups), or 3 to 4 ounces *each* mozzarella (preferably whole milk) and Italian Fontina, freshly grated (or more to taste)
1 tablespoon minced fresh basil or oregano or 1 teaspoon dried, crumbled
Freshly ground pepper

2 tablespoons freshly grated Parmesan cheese
1 to 2 tablespoons minced fresh basil, oregano or parsley

Prepare basic dough. Set aside to rise.

Place tomatoes in colander. Sprinkle with salt and let drain at least 30 minutes. Squeeze until completely dry (potato ricer works well). Roll tightly in cheesecloth or kitchen towels to remove any remaining moisture.

Position rack in center of oven and arrange baking stone or quarry tiles over top. Preheat oven to 425°F for 30 minutes. Shape pizza dough into 12-inch circle following Basic Pizza Dough directions. Brush dough with olive oil. Top with 1/4 cup Parmesan, half of mozzarella and all of reserved tomatoes, leaving 1/2-inch border. Sprinkle with 1 tablespoon fresh basil, pepper to taste and remaining mozzarella. Bake until crust browns, about 15 to 20 minutes.

Brush rim of pizza with olive oil. If tomatoes release liquid during cooking, pierce rim of pizza with sharp knife, then tilt to drain liquid through slit. Starting at slit, divide pizza into serving pieces with pizza cutter, scissors or serrated knife. Sprinkle with remaining 2 tablespoons Parmesan and 1 to 2 tablespoons fresh basil, oregano or parsley. Serve immediately.

Variations

Garnishes. Pizza can be garnished as desired. Uncooked sausage, onions, mushrooms, peppers, anchovies and olives should be added after mozzarella. Cooked sausage, salami, pepperoni and seafood should be added during last 3 to 5 minutes of baking.

Cheese and Tomato Pizza with Garlic. Separate 1 full head of garlic into individual unpeeled cloves, discarding any loose husks. Drop into pot of boiling water and simmer until tender when pierced with knife, about 20 minutes. Drain garlic well. Force through sieve to puree. Spread on pizza dough after brushing with olive oil. One teaspoon minced fresh garlic can be substituted for cooked garlic puree.

Cheese Pizza with Cooked Tomato Sauce. Heat 2 tablespoons olive oil in heavy saucepan over medium heat. Add 2 pounds tomatoes (about 6 medium), peeled, seeded and chopped, and 1/4 teaspoon minced fresh garlic. Cover and cook to render juices, about 10 minutes. Transfer tomatoes to strainer set over medium bowl and let drain, gently pressing down occasionally, about 10 minutes. Return tomato juices to pan and boil until reduced to 1/4 cup, about 15 minutes. Blend with tomatoes. Cool. Season sauce with salt, pepper and herbs to taste. If sauce is too acidic, add pinch of sugar.

Chez Panisse's Mediterranean Pizza with Zucchini and Eggplant

Makes one 12-inch pizza

Basic Pizza Dough for 12-inch pizza (see page 101)

1 medium tomato (about 6 to 7 ounces), seeded, juiced and diced
3/4 teaspoon salt

Olive oil for deep frying
1 3-ounce Japanese eggplant or 3-ounce section of eggplant, thinly sliced diagonally

1 tablespoon olive oil
4 ounces zucchini, thinly sliced

Olive oil
1/2 medium-size sweet red onion (about 3 ounces), thinly sliced
1 large garlic clove, minced
2 ounces *each* freshly grated mozzarella cheese (preferably whole milk) and Italian Fontina cheese (1 cup)

Salt and freshly ground pepper
3 tablespoons freshly grated Parmesan cheese
2 tablespoons minced fresh parsley
1 tablespoon minced fresh chives

Prepare basic dough. Set aside to rise.

Place tomato in colander. Sprinkle with salt and let drain at least 30 minutes. Squeeze until completely dry (potato ricer works well). Roll tightly in cheesecloth or kitchen towel to remove any remaining moisture.

Heat olive oil for deep frying in heavy skillet. Add eggplant and brown on both sides, about 3 minutes. Remove eggplant from skillet using slotted spoon and drain or paper towels.

Heat 1 tablespoon olive oil in heavy small skillet over medium-high heat. Add zucchini and stir-fry until heated through, about 3 minutes.

Position rack in center of oven and arrange baking stone or quarry tiles over top. Preheat oven to 425°F for 30 minutes. Shape pizza dough into 12-inch circle following Basic Pizza Dough directions. Brush with olive oil. Sprinkle with onion and garlic, leaving 1/2-inch border. Sprinkle mozzarella and Fontina over onion, filling in any spaces on dough. Top with tomato. Bake 15 minutes. Ring eggplant around pizza 2 inches in from edge. Overlap zucchini on inside edge of eggplant. Bake until crust browns, about 5 more minutes.

Brush rim of pizza with olive oil. Sprinkle zucchini and eggplant with salt and pepper to taste. Divide pizza into serving pieces with pizza cutter, scissors or serrated knife. Sprinkle with Parmesan, parsley and chives. Serve hot.

Chez Panisse's Mexicana Pizza

The peppers can be varied to suit seasonal availability and desired degree of piquancy. If only hot serranos or jalapeños can be found, it may be preferable to limit chilies to 2 ounces and substitute sweet bells for the remaining 16 to 18 ounces. For a more colorful dish, choose a variety of chilies.

Makes one 12-inch pizza

- Basic Pizza Dough for 12-inch pizza (see page 101)
- 1 medium tomato (about 6 to 7 ounces), seeded, juiced and diced
- 3/4 teaspoon salt
- 3 pasilla or poblano chilies (about 5 ounces)
- 3 long green mild chilies (about 4 ounces)
- 5 güero chilies (about 2 1/2 ounces)
- 2 medium-size red bell peppers (about 8 to 10 ounces)
- 1 tablespoon olive oil
- 1 1/2 teaspoons minced fresh oregano or 1/2 teaspoon dried, crumbled
- 1/4 teaspoon ground cumin
- 1 teaspoon Sherry vinegar or red wine vinegar
- Salt and freshly ground pepper
- Olive oil
- 1/2 medium-size sweet red onion (about 3 ounces), thinly sliced
- 1 large garlic clove, minced
- 2 ounces freshly grated *dry* Monterey Jack cheese (1/2 cup)
- 2 ounces freshly grated Monterey Jack cheese (1/2 cup)
- 4 ounces chorizo (optional)
- 2 tablespoons minced fresh parsley (garnish)
- Cilantro leaves (garnish)

Prepare basic dough. Set aside to rise.

Place tomato in colander. Sprinkle with salt and let drain at least 30 minutes. Squeeze until completely dry (potato ricer works well). Roll tightly in cheesecloth or kitchen towels to remove any remaining moisture.

Preheat broiler. Arrange pasilla, mild and güero chilies and red peppers in broiler pan. Roast 6 inches from heat source, turning until blackened on all sides. Transfer to plastic bag and steam 10 minutes. Peel chilies and peppers, discarding veins and seeds. Rinse, if necessary, and pat dry with paper towels. Slice into julienne. Heat olive oil in heavy skillet over medium heat. Add chilies and peppers, sprinkle with oregano and cumin and stir until warmed through, about 3 minutes. Blend in vinegar. Season with salt and freshly ground pepper to taste.

Position rack in center of oven and arrange baking stone or quarry tiles over top. Preheat oven to 425°F for 30 minutes. Shape pizza dough into 12-inch circle following Basic Pizza Dough directions. Brush with olive oil. Sprinkle with onion and garlic, leaving 1/2-inch border. Arrange chilies, peppers and tomato over onion. Combine dry and moist cheese and sprinkle over vegetables. Top with pieces of chorizo. Bake until crust browns, 15 to 20 minutes.

Brush rim of pizza with olive oil. Sprinkle top with parsley. Divide pizza into serving pieces with pizza cutter, scissors or serrated knife. Sprinkle cilantro leaves over pizza. Serve immediately.

Red Pepper and Italian Sausage Pizza

2 servings

- 2 medium-size red bell peppers
- 12 ounces hot Italian sausage
- 1/4 cup olive oil
- 2 cups sliced onion
- 1 tablespoon chopped fresh basil or 1 teaspoon dried, crumbled
- Salt and freshly ground pepper
- 1 large shaped Pizza Dough circle or 2 small circles*
- 4 ounces Monterey Jack cheese, shredded
- 2 ounces Parmesan cheese, freshly grated

Char peppers over gas flame or under broiler until skins blister and blacken. Place in plastic bag, seal tightly and let steam 10 minutes. Peel off skins and remove seeds. Cut peppers lengthwise into 1/4-inch strips. Set aside.

Preheat oven to 425°F. Remove sausage from casings. Cook in heavy large skillet over medium-high heat until no longer pink, stirring frequently, 8 to 10 minutes. Drain on paper towels.

Heat oil in another heavy large skillet over low heat. Add onion and bell peppers and cook until onion is soft and golden, stirring frequently, about 10 minutes. Add basil, salt and pepper. Let cool to room temperature.

Spread half of red pepper mixture on prepared dough circle(s). Top with half of grated cheese and sprinkle with half of sausage. Repeat layering. Bake until topping is bubbling and crust is golden brown, 15 to 20 minutes. Cut into wedges and serve immediately.

*Pizza Dough

This can be prepared up to one month ahead and frozen.

Makes one 12- to 14-inch or two 6-inch round pizzas

1 1/4 cups all purpose flour
1/4 cup whole wheat flour
1/2 teaspoon salt
1 teaspoon dry yeast
1/2 cup warm water (105°F to 115°F)
1 tablespoon olive oil

By hand: Mix flours and salt in large bowl. Make well in center. Sprinkle yeast into well. Pour about 2 tablespoons water over yeast and mix with fingertips until yeast dissolves. Pour in remaining water and olive oil. Starting from inside of circle, gradually incorporate flour into yeast mixture with fingers. Gather dough into ball. Transfer to lightly floured surface and knead until smooth and elastic, about 5 minutes. (If dough is too sticky, knead in additional flour 1 teaspoon at a time. If too dry, knead in more water a few drops at a time.)

With processor: Mix flours and salt using several on/off turns. Sprinkle yeast over water in small bowl and stir until dissolved. Add olive oil to yeast mixture. With machine running, add yeast mixture through feed tube and mix until dough just cleans side of bowl. Turn out onto lightly floured surface and knead until smooth and elastic, about 1 minute.

Oil large bowl. Transfer dough to bowl, turning to coat entire surface. Cover with dry cloth and let rise in warm draft-free area until doubled in volume, 1 1/2 to 2 hours.

Thirty minutes before baking, position rack in center of oven. Set baking stone on rack. Preheat oven to 425°F.

Punch dough down. Lightly flour thin wooden board (peel) or unrimmed baking sheet. Trace one 12- to 14-inch circle or two 6-inch circles in flour. Set dough (or half of dough for two 6-inch pizzas) in center of circle. Flatten with fingertips and spin while pushing out toward edge. Turn dough over and repeat procedure until circle is 1/4 inch thick. Pinch rim to form edge.

Arrange desired topping over dough. Slide pizza off peel or baking sheet onto stone. Bake according to instructions above.

Dough can also be baked on same sheet or formed and baked in pizza pan.

To ensure crisp crust, spray oven with water before baking pizza. Repeat procedure twice during baking time.

Mexican Pizza

8 appetizer servings

Pizza Dough

- 1 envelope dry yeast
- 1 teaspoon sugar
- 3/4 cup warm water (105°F to 115°F)

- 1 large garlic clove
- 1 small piece onion (1 ounce)
- 1 2/3 cups unbleached all purpose flour
- 1/2 cup masa harina
- 1 1/2 teaspoons salt
- 1 teaspoon Hungarian paprika
- Pinch of ground red pepper
- 1 tablespoon vegetable oil

Topping

- 1/4 cup fresh parsley leaves
- 2 large green onions (1 ounce total), cut into 1-inch pieces

- 12 ounces Monterey Jack cheese, chilled
- 4 ounces mozzarella cheese, chilled

- Cornmeal

- 5 tablespoons bottled taco sauce
- 1 medium onion (4 ounces), sliced and separated into rings
- 1/2 teaspoon salt
- Freshly ground pepper
- 1 medium-size green bell pepper (6 ounces), cored, seeded and sliced
- 1 3 1/2-ounce can mild or hot jalapeño peppers, drained and cut into julienne
- 1/2 teaspoon dried oregano, crumbled
- Crushed red pepper flakes (optional)
- 2 teaspoons vegetable oil

For dough: Combine yeast and sugar with warm water in small bowl. Let stand in warm place until foamy, about 10 minutes. Oil large mixing bowl.

Using food processor fitted with steel knife, mince garlic and onion by dropping through feed tube with machine running. Add flour, masa harina, salt, paprika and red pepper and mix 5 seconds. With machine running, pour yeast mixture through feed tube and mix 10 seconds. Add oil and mix until dough is smoothly and uniformly kneaded, about 40 seconds. Transfer to oiled bowl, turning to coat all surfaces. Cover with damp towel and let stand in warm, draft-free area until doubled in volume, about 1 1/2 hours.

Meanwhile, prepare topping: Mince parsley and green onion in processor. Leave in work bowl.

Insert shredder and shred cheeses using light pressure. Reinsert steel knife and mix using 10 on/off turns. Leave in work bowl.

About 15 minutes before baking, position rack in center of oven and preheat to 425°F. Cover rack with unglazed quarry tiles if available. Grease 15-inch pizza pan or baking sheet large enough to accommodate 15-inch circle. Sprinkle lightly with cornmeal.

To assemble, roll dough out on lightly floured surface into circle 16 inches in diameter and about 1/4 inch thick. Wrap dough over rolling pin and unroll onto pan. Pinch up edges to form 1/2-inch rim. Spread taco sauce over dough. Arrange onion rings evenly over sauce. Sprinkle with 1/4 teaspoon salt and some freshly ground pepper. Sprinkle cheese mixture over onions all the way to rim, pressing gently. Arrange green pepper over cheese and dot with jalapeños. Sprinkle with oregano, remaining 1/4 teaspoon salt, freshly ground pepper and red pepper flakes. Drizzle with oil. Bake until cheese is golden brown, about 20 minutes. Let stand 5 minutes before cutting into wedges.

Pizza can be assembled ahead, baked 3/4 through, removed from pan, cooled and frozen (wrap tightly). To reheat, set unthawed pizza on baking sheet in cold oven. Set temperature to 425°F and bake until heated through, about 25 minutes.

Tomato-Potato Pissaladière

A potato-studded version of the classic pizza from the south of France.

Makes one 11 × 14-inch pizza

Rosemary-Garlic Crust

- 1 envelope dry yeast
- 1 teaspoon sugar
- 1/2 cup warm water (105°F to 115°F)
- Olive oil
- 2 cups (or more) unbleached all purpose flour
- 2 tablespoons olive oil
- 1 tablespoon minced fresh rosemary leaves or 1 teaspoon dried, crumbled
- 2 teaspoons minced garlic
- 1 teaspoon salt

Topping

- 7 tablespoons olive oil
- 1 teaspoon fresh thyme leaves
- 3/4 teaspoon fresh oregano leaves
- 2 medium baking potatoes, peeled, sliced paper-thin and patted dry (about 3 1/2 cups); do not wash
- 1 pound onions, very thinly sliced (about 4 cups)
- 1 teaspoon sugar
- 1 large garlic clove, minced
- 2 tablespoons capers, rinsed and drained
- 4 anchovies, minced
- 1 1/2 pounds medium-size ripe tomatoes
- 20 small Niçoise olives (optional)

For crust: Sprinkle yeast and 1/2 teaspoon sugar over 1/4 cup water in bowl of heavy-duty mixer fitted with dough hook. Stir until yeast dissolves. Cover and let stand until foamy, 10 minutes.

Coat large bowl with olive oil. Mix 1 cup flour, remaining 1/4 cup water, 2 tablespoons olive oil, rosemary, garlic, salt and remaining 1/2 teaspoon sugar into yeast mixture. Blend in remaining 1 cup flour until dough is soft, smooth and cleans sides of bowl (if dough is too moist, blend in more flour 1 tablespoon at a time). Knead dough until elastic, about 5 minutes. (Dough can also be prepared by hand.) Add dough to oiled bowl, turning to coat entire surface. Cover with plastic, then towel. Let stand in warm draft-free area until doubled, about 1 hour.

For topping: Blend 3 tablespoons olive oil, thyme and oregano in small bowl. Heat remaining 4 tablespoons olive oil in heavy large skillet over medium heat. Add potatoes in batches in single layer and cook 5 minutes per side. Remove with slotted spoon and drain on paper towels. Add onions and cook until softened, stirring occasionally, about 5 minutes. Mix in sugar and garlic and cook until onions are pale golden, stirring occasionally, about 20 minutes. Blend in capers and anchovies and cook 2 minutes. Cool mixture to room temperature.

Just before using, cut tomatoes in half. Squeeze to extract seeds and juice. Slice halves into rounds 1/4 inch thick.

Position rack in center of oven and preheat to 375°F. Lightly oil 11 × 14-inch metal baking pan with shallow sides. Punch dough down. Turn out onto work surface and knead 3 minutes. Roll dough out on waxed paper into rectangle large enough to fit bottom and sides of pan. Invert dough into pan, pressing gently. Spread onion mixture evenly over dough. Cover with alternating potato and tomato slices. Dot with olives if desired. Drizzle with herbed olive oil. Bake until vegetables are tender and crust is crisp and golden, 50 minutes. Serve warm or at room temperature.

Pizza Puffs

Especially easy open-face sandwiches for a quick lunch or supper. When made with tiny rounds of bread these puffs are great cocktail fare.

3 to 4 servings

- **2 egg whites**
- **2 teaspoons red wine vinegar**
- **8 ounces mozzarella cheese (well chilled), cut into 1-inch cubes**
- **1 small onion (2 ounces), halved**
- **1 ½-ounce piece pepperoni, halved**
- **½ teaspoon dried basil, crumbled**
- **¼ to ½ teaspoon dried oregano, crumbled**
- **¼ to ½ teaspoon dried oregano, crumbled**
- **¼ teaspoon salt (optional)**
- **⅓ cup mayonnaise (preferably homemade)**
- **⅓ cup tomato paste**
- **8 slices French or Italian bread, lightly toasted**

Using food processor fitted with steel knife, place egg whites in work bowl and whip 8 seconds. With machine running, pour vinegar through feed tube and continue processing until whites are stiff, about 45 seconds. Using rubber spatula, gently transfer egg whites to 1-quart mixing bowl; do not wash out work bowl.

Combine cheese, onion, pepperoni, basil, oregano and salt in work bowl and blend 10 seconds, stopping once to scrape down sides of work bowl. Add mayonnaise and blend 5 seconds. Add ¼ of egg whites and mix using 2 on/off turns. Add remaining egg whites. Run spatula around inside of work bowl, then blend using 3 on/off turns. Run spatula around inside of work bowl again. Mix using 1 more on/off turn.

Preheat broiler. Spread 2 teaspoons tomato paste over each slice of bread. Mound ¼ cup cheese mixture on each. Arrange on baking sheet. Broil 6 inches from heat source until tops are puffed and golden brown, about 3½ to 4 minutes. Serve immediately.

Stove-Top Pizza

Vary the toppings for these pizzas according to what you have on hand. Hard sausage, pepperoni, cooked hamburger and diced ham are all good, and you may want to include fresh-sliced tomatoes and fresh or canned mushrooms.

Makes two 12-inch pizzas

- **1 8-ounce can tomato sauce**
- **1 6-ounce can tomato paste**
- **1 tablespoon minced onion**
- **1 tablespoon minced dried mushrooms**
- **1 teaspoon dried oregano, crumbled**
- **Dash of hot pepper sauce**
- **Salt and freshly ground pepper**
- **1 16¾-ounce package hot roll mix**
- **Toppings of your choice**
- **1 pound mozzarella cheese, sliced, or ½ cup freshly grated Parmesan cheese**

Combine first 6 ingredients with salt and pepper to taste in saucepan. Bring to boil, reduce heat and simmer 20 minutes.

Meanwhile, line 2 heavy 12-inch skillets with well-greased foil. Prepare hot roll mix according to package directions. Divide dough between skillets and press onto bottom. Spoon tomato sauce evenly over dough and cover with desired toppings. Finish with cheese. Cover and cook over very low heat until cheese bubbles and crust is done, about 20 minutes.

Fruited Cheese Pizza

A delicious novelty: pizza for dessert!

12 servings

Rich Yeast Crust

1 tablespoon dry yeast
Pinch of sugar
¼ cup warm milk (105°F to 115°F)

3 cups all purpose flour
¼ cup sugar
½ teaspoon salt
½ cup (1 stick) unsalted butter, room temperature
3 eggs

Cheese Topping

2 cups cream cheese or ricotta cheese
½ cup sugar
2 egg yolks
3 tablespoons all purpose flour
2 tablespoons sour cream
1 tablespoon finely grated orange peel
1 teaspoon vanilla
Pinch *each* of salt, cardamom and mace
2 tablespoons sugar

Strawberry halves
Halved and pitted red and green grapes
Peeled and sliced bananas, papayas, kiwis, peaches, plums or nectarines
1 10-ounce jar apricot jam or currant jelly, melted

For crust: Sprinkle yeast and pinch of sugar into milk in small bowl; stir to dissolve. Let stand until foamy and proofed, about 10 minutes.

Grease large bowl. Combine 2½ cups flour, ¼ cup sugar and salt in another large bowl. Make well in center. Add yeast mixture, butter and eggs to well and blend until smooth. Gradually draw flour from inner edge of well into center until all flour is incorporated. Turn dough out onto work surface. Knead in remaining ½ cup flour, then continue kneading until dough is smooth and elastic, about 10 minutes. Add dough to prepared bowl, turning to coat entire surface. Let rise in warm draft-free area until doubled in volume, about 1¾ hours.

Grease 16-inch pizza pan.* Punch dough down. Roll dough out to circle ¼ to ⅛ inch thick. Fit into pan, pressing onto sides. Let dough rise in warm area until puffy, about 20 minutes.

Position rack in lower third of oven and preheat to 350°F.

For topping: In large bowl of electric mixer beat cheese, ½ cup sugar, yolks, flour, sour cream, peel, vanilla, salt and spices until smooth. Spoon into unbaked shell, spreading evenly. Sprinkle with 2 tablespoons sugar. Bake until crust is browned and filling is set, about 35 minutes. Cool completely in pan on rack.

Decorate pizza with fruit. Brush with melted jam. Serve within 5 hours.

*If unavailable, 2 shallow 11-inch tart pans with removable bottoms can be used. Dough can also be shaped into 4 individual pizzas, each 6½ inches in diameter.

Index

Arborio Rice (Risotto Milanese), 4
Anchovy (Anchoiade), with Mortadella and Olives, 99
Artichoke Hearts, Pasta with, 26
Artichoke Linguine, 26
Asparagus, Spaghetti with, 25

Balinese Fried Noodles (Bakmi Goreng), 92
Barbecued Pork, 94
Basic
- Pasta, Processor, 2
- Pasta, Semolina, 2
- Pizza Dough, 101
- Tomato Sauce, 38
- Tomato Sauce, Valentino's, 36

Basil, Fresh, Sauce for Lemon Tagliolini, 27
Basil Tomato Pasta, 7
Béchamel Sauce, Herbed Tomato, 18
Beef-Pasta Salad with Snow Peas and Cauliflower, 84
Belgian Endive. *See* Fettuccine con Radicchio
Blanquette de Veau with Fresh Pasta, 72
Breadcrumb Sauce (alla Briciolata), Pasta with, 22
Broccoli-Orzo Salad, Spicy, 27
Broccoli Pasta, 3
Broccoli Taglierini, 26
Butter, Peppered Sauce, New Orleans, 12
Butter Tomato Sauce, 40
Butterfly (Bows) Pasta. *See* Farfalle

Calistoga Inn's Fettuccine with Smoked Salmon, 60
Cantonese. *See also* Oriental
Cantonese Seafood Noodle, 95
Capellini with Fresh Tomato and Basil Sauce, 42
Capellini Primavera La Camelia (with Vegetables), 44
Carrot Fettuccine with Carrots, Scallops and Vermouth, 61
Carrot Pasta, 3
Cheese and Tomato Pizza di Bufalo, 105
Chez Panisse's Mediterranean Pizza with Zucchini and Eggplant, 106
Chez Panisse's Mexicana Pizza, 107
Chicken
- and Buckwheat Noodles in Peanut Sauce, 90
- Golden with Saffron Pasta, 69
- -Liver Walnut Filling for Green Ravioli, 70
- and Pesto, Spinach Fettuccine with, 68
- "In the Pink" with Four Cheeses, Pasta with, 68
- with Rice Noodles (Pancit), Filipino, 91
- Salad. *See* Pasta-Beef Salad with Snow Peas and Cauliflower
- Spaghetti, 69
- Thai Fried Noodles, 94

Chinese. *See also* Oriental
Chinese Noodles and Vegetables, Marinated, 89
Chive-Lemon Tortelli with Scallop Mousse, 62
Clam Sauce, Fresh, Lemon Tagliolini with, 57
Clam Sauce, New England, Linguine with, 56
Classic Tomato Sauce, 39
Clove Sauce, Spicy, 41
Coriander-Cumin Tomato Sauce, 40
Crab and Pasta Genovese, 58
Crab (King) Fettuccine, 57
Cream Sauce for Orange Pappardelle, 30

Dessert Pizza, Fruited Cheese, 112
Dough. *See* Pasta, Pizza

Easy
- Fettuccine, 14
- Italian Pizza, 98
- Linguine Romano, 70

Egg Pasta, Spinach and Herbs, 37
Eggplant and Macaroni Casserole, 27
Eggplant and Tomato Topping, Pasta with, 28
Endive, Belgian. *See* Fettuccine con Radicchio

Farfalle (Butterflies, Bows) Pasta
- Green Pea, 5
- Green Pea, with Peas, Green Onion and Mint, 33

Fettuccine
- About Cutting, 3
- Broccoli Taglierini, 26
- Carbonara, Vegetable, 45
- Carrot with Carrots, Scallops and Vermouth, 61
- Crab (King), 56
- Easy, 14
- au Gorgonzola, 15
- with Gorgonzola Cream Sauce, 15
- Green, with Prosciutto and Peas, 33
- with Mascarpone Sauce, 16
- con Radicchio, 35
- with Smoked Salmon, 60
- Spinach, with Chicken and Pesto, 68
- Spinach (Pasta Allegra), 13
- Verdi (Green) Capriccio, 79
- Zelda's, 14

Filipino Chicken with Rice Noodles (Pancit), 91
Food Processor. *See* Processor
Francis Coppola's Fusilli alla Pappone, 44
Fresh
- Pasta, 73
- Tomato and Basil Sauce, Capellini with, 42

Fresh (*continued*)
Tomato and Green Olive Sauce, 44
Tomato Sauce, Uncooked, 39
Tomato Soup with Spinach Ravioli, 58
Fried. *See also* Stir-Fried
Fried Rice Noodles with Barbecued Pork, 93
Fruited Cheese Pizza, 112
Fukien Sesame Seed Sauce, 88
Fusilli (Spiral Macaroni)
alla Pappone, Francis Coppola's, 44
Pugliesi (Spinach Fusilli), 56
with Salsa Piccante, 22
Tricolored with Shrimp and Roasted Peppers, 64

Garden Sauce with Cottage Cheese, 14
Garganelli with Mushrooms, Sausage and Cream Sauce, 78
Garlic (Aglio), Pasta with, 41
Gnocchi
About, 4
Pumpkin with Walnut Cream Sauce, 10
Verde, Mrs. Sinatra's, 9
Goat Cheese, Pasta Ramekins with, 17
Gorgonzola
Cream Sauce, Fettuccine with, 15
au Pasta, 15
Sauce with Pasta, 15
Green Fettuccine. *See* Spinach Fettuccine
Green Onion Pasta, 8
Green Pasta with Leeks, 28
Green Pea Farfalle, 5
with Peas, Green Onion and Mint, 33
(Green) Peas and Prosciutto, Green Fettuccine with, 33
Green Ravioli with Chicken-Liver Walnut Filling, 70
Green and Red Pepper Lasagne, 50
Green Tomato Spaghetti with Red Tomato Sauce (alla Prematura), 47

Ham Salad. *See* Pasta-Beef Salad with Snow Peas and Cauliflower
Herb Pasta with Double Tomato Sauce, 42
Herb Pasta, Whole Wheat, 52
Herbed Tomato Sauce, 40
Homemade Spaghetti Sauce (Microwave), 84

Indonesian (Balinese) Soy Sauce (Kecap Manis), 92
Italian
Pizza, Easy, 98
Sausage and Red Pepper Pizza, 107
Tomato Sauce, Savory, 79

Kecap Manis (Indonesian Soy Sauce), 92

Lasagne. *See also* Piccagge
About Cutting, 3
Green and Red Pepper (di Peperoni), 50
Green and White (Verdi e Bianchi), 18
Meatball-Stuffed, 85
Pesto, 75
Red, White and Green (Vincisgrassi), 74
Semolina, 86
Spinach, Quick, 74
Leek and Shrimp Pizza with Feta Cheese, 104
Leeks, Green Pasta with, 28
Lemon Tagliolini, 5
with Fresh Basil Sauce, 27
with Fresh Clam Sauce, 57
Ligurian Walnut Pesto, 24
Linguine. *See also* Spaghetti
Artichoke, 26
Crab and Pasta Genovese, 58
with Freshly Grated Nutmeg and Pepper, 12
with New England Clam Sauce, 56
with Paprika Sauce, 35
Pasta Riviera (Tomato-Orange), 81
Pasta with Artichoke Hearts, 26
Romano, Easy, 70
Lobster and Basil, Red Pepper Pasta with, 59

Macaroni (Maccheroni). *See also* Garganelli, Shells
and Eggplant Casserole, 27
with Sauce Spiga, 34
Maltagliati and Mushrooms, Cream of Vegetable Soup with, 53
Marinated Chinese Noodles and Vegetables, 89
Mascarpone Sauce, Pasta with, 16
Meatball-Stuffed Lasagne (Sagne Chine), 85
Mediterranean Pizza with Zucchini and Eggplant, Chez Panisse's, 106
Mediterranean Sauce for Pasta, 29
Mexican Pizza, 109
Mexicana Pizza, Chez Panisse's, 107
Microwave Sauce, Homemade Spaghetti, 84
Minestrone Soup, 52
Mozzarella and Tomato Sauce, 43
Mrs. Sinatra's Gnocchi Verde, 9
Mushroom(s)
Filling for Ravioli, 82
Pizza with Garlic Butter, 98
Sauce, Piccagge with, 30
Sausage and Cream Sauce, Garganelli with, 78
Spinach and Cream Sauce for Orange Pappardelle, 30
-Tomato Sauce for Meatball-Stuffed Lasagne, 85
and Zucchini Topping for Pasta, 31

New Orleans Peppered Butter Sauce, 12
Niçoise Pizza, 104
Niçoise Sauce for Shell Pasta, 66
Noodles. *See also* Rice Noodles
About, 4
Balinese, Fried (Bakmi Goreng), 92
Buckwheat and Chicken in Peanut Sauce, 90
Cold with Peanut Butter Sauce, 91
Marinated Chinese and Vegetables, 89
Oriental, 88
Oriental, Sesame Seed Sauce for, 88
Paglia e Fieno (Straw and Hay), 12
Rice (Pancit), Chicken with, 91
Spinach, Creamy, 13
and Spinach, Ukrainian, 36
Szechuan Dan Dan, 88
Thai Fried (Pad Thai), 94
Transparent, Stir-Fried, 93

Olive, Green and Fresh Tomato Sauce, 44
Onion. *See also* Green Onion
Onion and Pea Sauce for Strichetti, 32
Orange Pappardelle, 6
with Fresh Spinach, Mushroom and Cream Sauce, 30
Oriental
Balinese Fried Noodles (Bakmi Goreng), 92
Buckwheat Noodles (Soba) and Chicken in Peanut Sauce, 90
Cantonese Seafood Noodle, 95
Filipino Chicken with Rice Noodles (Pancit), 91
Fried Rice Noodles with Barbecued Pork, 93
Noodles, 88
Noodles (Salad) with Peanut Butter Sauce, Cold, 91
Noodles, Sesame Seed Sauce for, 88
Noodles, Szechuan Dan Dan, 88
Noodles, Transparent, Stir-Fried, 93
Pasta Salad, Cafe Mariposa, 89

Soy Sauce, Kecap Manis, 92
Thai Fried Noodles, 94
Orzo-Broccoli Salad, 27
Orzo, Pasta Pilaf, 12

Pansotti with Pesto, Tomatoes and Cream, 49
Pappardelle, Orange, 6
with Spinach, Mushroom and Cream Sauce, 30
with Rabbit Sauce Ligurian Style, 71
Paprika Sauce, Linguine with, 35
Pasta (Farinacei)
About (Tips and Techniques), 19
About Varieties, 4
con Aglio, 41
Allegra (Spinach Fettuccine), 13
with Artichoke Hearts, 26
Basic Processor, 2
Basic Semolina, 2
-Beef Salad with Snow Peas and Cauliflower, 84
with Breadcrumb Sauce (alla Briciolata), 22
Broccoli, 3
Capellini with Fresh Tomato and Basil Sauce, 42
Capellini Primavera La Camelia (with Vegetables), 44
Carrot, 3
and Crab Genovese, 58
Egg, Spinach and Herbs, 37
with Eggplant and Tomato Topping, 28
Farfalle, Green Pea, 5
Farfalle, Green Pea, with Peas, Green Onion and Mint, 33
Fettuccine. *See* Fettuccine
Fresh, 73
Fresh, Blanquette de Veau with, 72
Fusilli. *See* Fusilli
Garden (with Vegetables), 46
Garganelli with Mushrooms, Sausage and Cream Sauce, 78
Gnocchi Verde, Mrs. Sinatra's, 9
with Gorgonzola Sauce, 15
Green, with Leeks, 28
Green Onion, 8
with Green Onion, Herbed Tomato and Olive Topping, 45
Herb, with Double Tomato Sauce, 42
Lasagne. *See* Lasagne
Linguine. *See* Linguine
Macaroni. *See* Macaroni
Maltagliati and Mushrooms, Cream of Vegetable Soup with, 53
with Mascarpone Sauce, 16
with Mediterranean Sauce, 29
with Mushroom and Zucchini Topping, 31
Noodles. *See* Noodles
Orzo-Broccoli Salad, Spicy, 27
(Orzo) Pilaf, 12
Pansotti with Pesto, Tomatoes and Cream, 49
Pappardelle. *See* Pappardelle
Piccagge with Mushroom Sauce, 30
Ramekins with Goat Cheese, 17
Ravioli. *See* Ravioli
Red Pepper, 6
Red Pepper with Lobster and Basil, 59
Rice Flour, Shrimp and Feta with, 64
Rigatoni del Curato (Mushrooms and Bacon), 80
Riviera (Tomato-Orange), 81
Rotolo, Stuffed with Spinach Filling, 76
Saffron, 7
Saffron, Chicken with, 69
Salad, Oriental, Cafe Mariposa, 89
Shell (small), with Niçoise Sauce, 66
with Shrimp and Vegetables, 65
del Sol (with Vegetables), 48
Spaghetti. *See* Spaghetti
Spinach. *See* Spinach Pasta, 66
Strichetti (Butterfly), with Onion and Pea Sauce, 32
Summer, About, 65
Taglierini, Broccoli, 26
Tagliolini. *See* Tagliolini; *see also* Linguine
Timbale with Chianti Vinaigrette, 19
Tomato Basil, 7
Tortelli, Chive-Lemon Filled with Scallop Mousse, 62
Tubular, with Chicken "In the Pink" with Four Cheeses, 68
Vegetable, 47
Whole Wheat Herb, 52
Ziti Salad with Sausage, 75
Pea(s) *See* Green Peas
Peanut Butter Sauce for Cold Noodles Salad, 91
Peanut Sauce, Chicken and Buckwheat Noodles in, 90
Penne. *See* Pasta, Tubular
Pepper, Green and Red, Lasagne, 50
Pepper, Red. *See* Red Pepper
Peppered Olive Sauce with Walnuts, 34
Pesto
and Chicken, Spinach Fettuccine with, 68
-Filled Won Ton Ravioli, 25
Lasagne, 75
Ligurian Walnut, 24
with Pimiento Sauce, 23
Pistachio, 23
Sauce, 23
Sauce for Pansotti, 49
Spinach, 24
Tomato with Garlic and Pimiento, 24
Piccagge with Mushroom Sauce (Sugo di Funghi), 30
Piccante Salsa with Fusilli, 22
Pilaf, Pasta, 12
Pimiento Pesto, 23
Pine Nut and Raisin Vinaigrette, 36
Pissaladière, Tomato-Potato (Pizza), 110
Pistachio Pesto, 23
Pizza
About Preparing and Baking (Primer), 100–1
Anchoiade (Anchovy) with Mortadella and Olives, 99
Cheese (Bufalo Mozzarella) and Tomato, 105; with variations, 105
Dough, 108
Dough, Basic, 101
Dough with Starter, 102; About Preparing, 102–3
Fruited Cheese, 112
Italian, Easy, 98
Mexican, 109
Mexicana, Chez Panisse's, 107
Mushroom with Garlic Butter, 98
Niçoise, 104
Pissaladière (Tomato-Potato), 110
Puffs, 111
Red Pepper and Italian Sausage, 107
Shrimp and Leek with Feta Cheese, 104
Steaming Method, 103
Stove-Top, 111
with Zucchini and Eggplant, Chez Panisse's Mediterranean, 106
Polenta, About, 4
Pork
Barbecued, 94
Barbecued, Fried Rice Noodles with, 93
Salad. *See* Pasta-Beef Salad with Snow Peas and Cauliflower
Potato-Tomato Pissaladière (Pizza), 110
Processor Pasta, Basic, 2
Prosciutto and Peas, Green Fettuccine with, 33
Pumpkin Gnocchi with Walnut Cream Sauce, 10

Quick Herbed Tomato Sauce, 38
Quick Spinach Lasagne, 74

Rabbit Sauce for Pappardelle, Ligurian Style, 71
Radicchio, Fettuccine con, 35
Raisin and Pine Nut Vinaigrette, 36

Ramekins, Pasta with Goat
Cheese, 17
Ravioli
About, 4; About Cutting, 3
al Burro, 16
Green with Chicken-Liver Walnut
Filling, 70
of Mushrooms with Pine Nuts,
Cured Ham and Cream, 82
Pasta Timbale with Chianti
Vinaigrette, 19
Spinach, Fresh Tomato Soup
with, 58
Won Ton, Pesto-Filled, 25
Raw. *See* Uncooked
Red Pepper
and Italian Sausage Pizza, 107
Pasta, 6
Pasta with Lobster and Basil, 59
-Tomato (Red on Red) Sauce, 35
Red on Red (Red Pepper-Tomato)
Sauce, 35
Rice Flour Pasta, Shrimp and Feta
with, 64
Rice Noodles, Fried with Barbecued
Pork, 93
Rice Noodles (Pancit), Chicken
with, Filipino, 91
Rigatoni. *See also* Pasta, Tubular
Rigatoni del Curato (Mushrooms
and Bacon), 80
Risotto Milanese, About, 4
Rotolo, Stuffed with Spinach
Filling, 76

Saffron Pasta, 7
Saffron Pasta, Chicken with, 69
Salad
Broccoli-Orzo, Spicy, 27
Chicken and Buckwheat Noodles
in Peanut Sauce, 90
Noodles, Cold with Peanut Butter
Sauce, 91
Pasta-Beef with Snow Peas and
Cauliflower, 84
Pasta, Oriental, Cafe
Mariposa, 89
Ziti with Sausage, 75
Salmon. *See* Smoked Salmon
Salsa Verde, 22
Sandwich, Pizza Puffs, 111
Sauce (Salsa)
Basil, Fresh, Lemon Tagliolini
with, 27
Breadcrumb (Briciolata), Pasta
with, 22
Chianti Vinaigrette for Pasta
Timbale, 19
Clam, Fresh, Lemon Tagliolini
with, 57
Clam, New England, Linguine
with, 56
Clove, Spicy, 41
Feta Cheese Dressing for Rice
Flour Pasta with Shrimp, 64
Garden with Cottage Cheese, 14
Gorgonzola Cream, Fettuccine
with, 15
Gorgonzola with Pasta, 15
Mascarpone for Pasta, 16
Mediterranean for Pasta, 29
Mushroom. *See* Mushrooms
Niçoise for Shell Pasta, 66
Onion and Pea for Strichetti, 32
Paprika, Linguine with, 35
Peanut Butter for Cold Noodles
Salad, 91
Peanut, Chicken and Buckwheat
Noodles in, 90
Peppered Butter, New Orleans, 12
Peppered Olive with Walnuts, 34
Pesto. *See* Pesto
Pine Nuts, Cured Ham and
Cream for Ravioli, 82
Rabbit for Pappardelle, Ligurian
Style, 71
Red on Red (Red Pepper-
Tomato), 35
Salsa Piccante, 22
Salsa Verde, 22
Sesame Seed, Fukien, 88
Shrimp and Feta Cheese, à la
Grecque, 63
Soy, Indonesian (Kecap Manis), 92
Spaghetti, Homemade
(Microwave), 84
Spiga, Macaroni, with, 34
Spinach, Mushroom and Orange
for Orange Pappardelle, 30
Tomato. *See* Tomato(es)
Tuna Mayonnaise, 66
Vinaigrette, Raisin and Pine
Nut, 36
Walnut Cream for Pumpkin
Gnocchi, 10
Sausage. *See* Italian Sausage
Savory Italian Tomato Sauce, 79
Scallop Mousse Filling for Chive-
Lemon Tortelli, 62
Scallops, Carrots and Vermouth,
Carrot Fettuccine with, 61
Szechuan. *See also* Oriental
Seafood. *See also* Name of Seafood
Seafood Noodle, Cantonese, 95
Semolina
Lasagne, 86
Pasta, About Cutting, 3
Pasta, Basic, 2
Sesame Seed Sauce, Fukien, 88
Shell Pasta (small) with Sauce
Niçoise, 66
Shells à la Thom, 79
Shrimp
and Feta Cheese Sauce à la
Grecque, 63
and Feta with Rice Flour
Pasta, 64
and Leek Pizza with Feta
Cheese, 104
and Roasted Peppers, Tricolored
Fusilli with, 64
and Vegetables, Pasta with, 65
Smoked Salmon, Fettuccine with,
Calistoga Inn's, 60
Smoked Salmon, Spaghetti with, 61
Soba, Japanese Buckwheat Noodles
and Chicken in Peanut Sauce, 90
Soups
Cream of Vegetable with
Mushrooms and
Maltagliati, 53
Fresh Tomato with Spinach
Ravioli, 58
Minestrone, 52
Soy Sauce, Indonesian (Kecap
Manis), 92
Spaghetti. *See also* Linguine
About, 4
with Asparagus, 25
Carbonara with Prosciutto, 81
Chicken, 69
Crab and Pasta Genovese, 58
Green Tomato with Red Tomato
Sauce, 47
Pasta Riviera, 81
Pasta with Shrimp and
Vegetables, 65
Sauce, 47; *See also* Sauce
Sauce, Homemade (Microwave),
84; with Smoked Salmon, 61
Spicy Broccoli-Orzo Salad, 27
Spicy Clove Sauce, 41
Spiga Sauce, Macaroni with, 34
Spinach
Fettuccine with Chicken and
Pesto, 68
Fettuccine (Pasta Allegra), 13
Fettuccine con Radicchio, 35
Fusilli Pugliesi, 56
and Herbs, Egg Pasta with, 37
Lasagne, Quick, 74
Mushroom and Cream Sauce for
Orange Pappardelle, 30
Noodles, Creamy, 13
and Noodles, Ukrainian, 36
Pasta with Tuna Mayonnaise, 66
Pesto, 24
Ravioli, Fresh Tomato Soup
with, 58
Spiral Macaroni. *See* Fusilli
Stir-Fried Transparent Noodles
(Sotanghon), 93
Stove-Top Pizza, 111
Straw and Hay (Noodles), 12
Strichetti with Onion and Pea
Sauce, 32
Stuffed Pasta. *See* Ravioli
Stuffed Rotolo (di Pasta
Ripieno), 76
Szechuan Dan Dan Noodles, 88

Taglierini, Broccoli, 26
Tagliolini. *See also* Linguine
Lemon, 5
Lemon, with Fresh Basil

Sauce, 27
Lemon, with Fresh Clam Sauce, 57
Tomato, 8
Tomato with Tomatoes, Mozzarella and Basil, 43
Verdi (Spinach) Gratinati, 83
Thai Fried Noodles (Pad Thai), 94
Timbale, Pasta with Chianti Vinaigrette, 19
Tomato(es)
Basil Pasta, 7
and Cheese Pizza di Bufalo, 105
and Eggplant Topping, Pasta with, 28
Fresh, Soup with Spinach Ravioli, 58
Green. *See* Green Tomato
Pesto with Garlic and Pimiento, 24
-Potato Pissaladière (Pizza), 110
Tagliolini, 8
Tagliolini with Tomatoes, Mozzarella and Basil, 43
Tomato Sauce
Basic, 38
Basic, Valentino's, 36
Butter, 40
Classic, 39
Coriander-Cumin, 40
Double, 42
Fresh and Basil, Capellini with, 42
Fresh and Green Olives, 44
Herbed, 40
Herbed Béchamel, 18
and Mozzarella, 43
Quick Herbed, 38
Red for Green Tomato Spaghetti, 47
-Red Pepper (Red on Red) Sauce, 35
Savory Italian, 79
Uncooked Fresh, 39
Topping for Pasta, Green Onion, Herbed Tomato and Kalamata Olives, 45
Tortelli, Chive-Lemon Filled with Scallop Mousse, 62
Tubular Pasta. *See* Pasta, Tubular
Tuna Mayonnaise, 66

Ukrainian Spinach and Noodles, 36
Uncooked Fresh Tomato Sauce, 39

Valentino's Basic Tomato Sauce, 36
Veal, Blanquette de Veau with Fresh Pasta, 72
Vegetable(s)
Fettuccine Carbonara, 45
Pasta, 47
and Pasta (Capellini Primavera), 44
and Pasta (del Sol), 48
and Shrimp, Pasta with, 65
Soup, Cream of, with Mushrooms and Maltagliati, 53
Soup (Minestrone), 52
and Chinese Noodles, Marinated, 89
Verde, Salsa, 22
Vinaigrette, Chianti, Sauce for Pasta Timbale, 19
Vinaigrette, Raisin and Pine Nut, 36
Vincisgrassi, Red, White and Green Lasagne, 74

Walnut Cream Sauce for Pumpkin Gnocchi, 10
Walnut Pesto, Ligurian, 24
Whole Wheat Herb Pasta, 52

Zelda's Fettuccine, 14
Ziti. *See also* Pasta, Tubular
Ziti Salad with Sausage, 75
Zucchini and Mushroom Topping for Pasta, 31

Credits and Acknowledgments

The following people contributed the recipes included in this book:

Adriano's, Los Angeles, California
Al Forno, Providence, Rhode Island
Al Tartufo, Salsomaggiore, Italy
The Apple Orchard, Ipswich, Massachusetts
Arrows, Ogunquit, Maine
Nancy Verde Barr
Terry Bell
Susan Biggs
Shanna Breen
Jennifer Brennan
Giuliano Bugialli
Zenaida Cacdac
Cafe Annie, Houston, Texas
Cafe Mariposa, Salt Lake City, Utah
Biba Caggiano
Calistoga Inn, Calistoga, California
Anna Teresa Callen
Guy Calluaud
Larry and Vicki Cansler
Roxanne Chan
Ginger Chang
Nona Chern
Mary Beth Clark
Peter and Susan Coe
Claudette Cole
Francis Coppola
Da Berti, Milan, Italy
Joe Famularo
Helen Feingold
Mary Gavin-Loughlin
Cora Gemil
Yvonne Gill
Peggy Glass
Phyllis Gorenstein
Freddi Greenberg
Gretchen's Of Course, Seattle, Washington
Hotel Villa Cipriani, Asolo, Italy
Bill Hughes
Louise Imperiale
Beverly Jackson
Roger Jaloux
Mary Ellen Jones
Jane Helsel Joseph
Linda Kamerman
Barbara Karoff
Lynne Kasper
Barbara Kleinman
Jim Kronman
La Camelia, New York, New York
Lanterna Blu, Imperia, Italy
Faye Levy
Johnny Low
Lucia's Pizza Restaurant, Fremont, California
Abby Mandel
Mary Manilla
Ivy Elinoff Marwil
Richard McCullough
Carmela Meely
Michael's, Santa Monica, California
Iris and Allan Mink
Jinx and Jefferson Morgan
Morgan's Lake Place, Bellevue, Washington
Doris Muscatine
Dale and Susie Pierson
Thelma Pressman
Lucy Rice
Margaret and Franco Romagnoli
Neil Romanoff
Bonnie Rothenberg
Rosalie Saferstein
San Marco, New York, New York
Elizabeth Schneider
Edena Sheldon
Elizabeth Sheley
Mrs. Frank Sinatra
Lucille Stakee
Gregory Usher
Valentino, Santa Monica, California
Venezia, Toronto, Ontario
Diane Ward
Jan Weimer
Alice Welsh
Audrey White
Yenching Palace, Washington, D.C.

Additional text was supplied by:
Anthony Dias Blue, *Pasta (Farinacei)*
Biba Caggiano, *Tips and Techniques*
Abby Mandel, *Summer Pastas*
Jan Weimer, *Pizza Primer*

The Knapp Press
is a wholly owned subsidiary of
KNAPP COMMUNICATIONS CORPORATION.
Chairman and Chief Executive Officer: Cleon T. Knapp
President: H. Stephen Cranston
Senior Vice-Presidents:
Betsy Wood Knapp (*MIS Electronic Media*)
Harry Myers (*Magazine Group Publisher*)
William J. N. Porter (*Corporate Product Sales*)
Paige Rense (*Editorial*)

Editor, Bon Appétit: Marilou Vaughan
Art Director, Bon Appétit: Bernard Rotondo
Associate Editor, The Knapp Press: Patricia Connell
Rights and Permissions Coordinator: Karen Legier
Indexer: Rose Grant

Composition by Publisher's Typography

This book is set in Sabon, a face designed by Jan Teischold in 1967 and based on early fonts engraved by Garamond and Granjon.